Essays on Kushner's Angels

Essays on Kushner's Angels

Edited by Per Brask

Blizzard Publishing
Winnipeg • Buffalo

Essays on Kushner's Angels first published 1995 by Blizzard Publishing Inc.
73 Furby Street, Winnipeg, Canada R3C 2A2.

Distributed in the United States by General Distribution Services,
85 River Rock Dr., Unit 202, Buffalo, NY 14207-2170.

"Tony Kushner Speaks Out." reprinted courtesy of Body Positive, Inc. of New
York; "Historical Revue and Dance of Death." reprinted courtesy of *Theater
heute*, Germany.

Cover photo: *Self Portrait / The Fall from Grace (excerpt)* by Simon Glass.
Cover design by Otium. Printed for Blizzard Publishing in Canada by Friesen
Printers.

5 4 3 2

Blizzard Publishing gratefully acknowledges the support of the
Manitoba Arts Council and the Canada Council to its publishing program.

Cataloguing in Publication Data

Main entry under title:
Essays on Kushner's Angels
  ISBN 0-921368-57-7
1. Kushner, Tony. Angels in America   I. Brask, Per K., 1952–

PS3561.U778A857 1995   812'.54   C95-920183-1

Table of Contents

Acknowledgements

I would like to thank Anna Synenko and Peter Atwood for asking me to embark on this project; the writers for their contributions; Tonia Farell at the Joyce Ketay Agency for her help; Patty Hawkins for her assistance on Bent Holm's article; Linwood DeLong for his assistance on Franz Wille's article; and to Carol Matas for her inexhaustible encouragement.

Foreword

by Per Brask

During the 1980s, the United States (and a good many other places in the Western world) witnessed the victory of neo-conservative supply-side economics with their attendant political and cultural rise of intolerance towards differently-thinking people. Most frightening about this process was (and still is) the basic cultural assumption held by many neo-cons that ambitious middle class white heterosexual males (or women behaving just like them) were the true heirs to whatever power was to be had in a rapidly changing world. And, though only very few people in, say, 1985–86 could have predicted the eventual and complete collapse of the Soviet empire, there was a vigorous sense that, as in the fifties, the true enemies to the glorious neo-con future were not really to be found across the seas but rather that they could be found within and that they should be fought like a virus.

In this context, Tony Kushner introduces us to his angels. History is on the move and so are the angels. Every character in *Angels in America* is in one way or another an angel for someone else. Everyone presents some redeeming moment, brings an important message to someone else. And every character desires a blessing, more life. Angels populate these plays, from the angel crashing through Prior's ceiling, to the Angel of Death leaving marks on Prior's skin, to the

PER BRASK studied dramaturgy at the University of Aarhus, Denmark and is Professor of Theatre at the University of Winnipeg. His books include *Drama Contemporary: Scandinavia*; *Double Danish* and *Aboriginal Voices: Amerindian, Inuit and Sami Theatre* (with William Morgan).

fallen angel, the Lucifer-like Roy Cohn. And even he, this darkest of the angels, is depicted in some way as being pure. His desire to be a father for Joe, to be a person who opens doors, is clearly not merely a tactic to have someone on his side in Washington. After all, in that case he wouldn't have needed Joe. Any ambitious stooge would have sufficed. But it is Joe Roy wants. And so we see, even Roy is capable of love, that most angelic of emotions.

If there is any angelic force missing in these plays, it is the avenging angel. Unless we take this to be the departed God. God avenging Himself, by leaving, by showing His absence.

However, if everyone in the play has angelic potential—fallen or otherwise—then Prior's final speech in *Perestroika* sensibly and consistently makes this potential available to the audience as well. We too, like the characters, are angelic and can be the bearers of hope and change.

In all instances Kushner has managed to create characters who are in no way satisfied with their given circumstances. No one provides a model for a contented, happy life. All of them reach for a better future, a goal, the hope that things do not need to remain the way they are pervades their basic assumptions. Again, even this includes Roy, though he would like nothing better than to return to his moment of glory when he caused the deaths of the Rosenbergs. Like a fallen angel, his desires for a better future reach backwards. He cannot look beyond.

What then seems to be Kushner's cure for the dissatisfaction his characters (and one must assume a good deal of his audience) suffer? When I saw the plays, George C. Wolfe's production in New York, and when I read them, I could not help but feel via Kushner's dramaturgy, that more life, blessing, also means more imagination. In a way, the plays are written according to the most traditional playwriting advice: that a play's main theme must reverberate throughout, that is, in some manner be present at every moment and reflected in all its characters. Kushner's genius, however, is that he is able to join traditional playwriting technique with an imaginative non-realistic theatrical universe which calls attention to its own inventiveness. In this way Kushner is not, in my reading, Brechtian in his use of the stage as metaphor. Rather, he seems very sensitive to the archetypes at play in neo-con times and his sharp sense of irony allows him to focus on the contrast between the mean-spirited imagination played out during the Reagan/Bush reigns and the different kind of life that would be possible with a more open-ended and playful imagination. In other words, Kushner's plays seem to suggest that the more literal the mind the narrower life's possibilities, the more fertile the imagination the more accepting it is of difference. Broadening the imagination, however, must include realizing that what the imagination produces is imaginative—as Kushner demonstrates by exposing the wires. Brecht, too, would have wanted the wires exposed, in order to avoid what he saw as the audience's narcotized involvement in the story. Kushner, on the other hand, seems to want the wires exposed in order to recognize the continual flow of the imagination, which of course is not an opposition to Brecht's notion but it does cause a different effect— Kushner's imagination effect, to coin a term.

The articles collected in this volume represent an attempt to provide a look at *Angels in America* from North American, European, and Australian perspectives; for readers to get a sense of how these amazing plays have fared in different contexts in the Western world where they have been widely recognized as heralding a renewed political theatre, a theatre that exposes the angel of history.

—Per Brask

Tony Kushner
Speaks Out

Interview by
Patrick Pacheco

Tony Kushner Speaks Out On AIDS, Angels, Activism & Sex in the Nineties

by Patrick Pacheco

While over the past decade AIDS has inspired a number of works of art, Tony Kushner's epic play *Angels in America* elevates dramatic treatment of the crisis to a provocative and unprecedented level, embracing both personal and national themes. No playwright in history has redefined Gay culture to the extent that Kushner does, setting his themes of loss, betrayal, forgiveness, and grace within the rapacious Reagan era. Divided into two parts, *Millennium Approaches* and *Perestroika*, the seven-hour-long epic is also a rollicking good tale, following, among many different characters, the adventures of Prior Walter, a cater-waiter drag queen living with AIDS who has been singled out to be a prophet. His bravery in the face of illness and the abandonment by his lover, a law clerk named Louis, is contrasted with the cynicism of another character, Roy Cohn, the self-hating, right-wing power broker who died of AIDS, and who in the play champions a closeted Mormon lawyer saddled with a valium-popping wife. All these lives intertwine in a daring, unsentimental mix of cosmic fantasy and kitchen-sink drama as moving as it is electrifying. *Millennium* won the Pulitzer prize and five Tony awards this year, including the award for best play.

Used with permission of *The Body Positive Magazine*, a publication of Body Positive, Inc. of New York, an AIDS service organization. This interview first appeared in *The Body Positive* September, 1993.

Perestroika opens in October and will play in rep with *Millennium* at the Walter Kerr Theatre. Kushner was hiding out, furiously reworking *Perestroika* for its debut when Patrick Pacheco contacted him for this exclusive *Body Positive* interview. Though he's turned down most other requests, Tony Kushner gave hours of his time to *Body Positive* for a wide-ranging chat unsparing in its honesty and insight.

Patrick Pacheco: What is it you'd like to say to PWAs? Do you have a message for them?

Tony Kushner: I don't write plays with messages, so I don't know how to answer that question without sounding like an idiot. The last thing anybody with AIDS needs is to be lectured to.

When I started work on *Millennium* in 1988, a lot of what I was reading and seeing about AIDS was using the illness as a dramatic device, *Camille*-type model, a way of getting a guaranteed tearjerker finish. It was important to me to create a character with AIDS who was not passive, who did not die at the end, but whose illness was treated realistically. So it wasn't just one lesion on the shoulder and then a little coughing fit and then he dies in time for the surviving lover to make a moving little speech that gets everybody in the theatre to cry and then leave feeling uplifted.

If you're going to deal with a biological problem, you have to deal with the biology. So there's a good deal of time spent in *Millennium* with Prior [the cater-waiter drag queen character who has AIDS] enumerating his symptoms and speaking very specifically of what he is going through; that was modelled on what several of my friends had gone through. I follow the same line of reasoning with Roy [Cohn, also a character] in *Perestroika*, trying to be true to the course of the illness in terms of what was available in 1985.

The play isn't intended to tell seropositive people or PWAs that they should be doing this or that. I've seen people do the most heroic things in dealing with this illness; and it's changed a lot of what I understand about courage and bravery and the places it comes from. And I hope the plays reflect that.

PP: When you started *Angels* had you taken an HIV test?

TK: I hadn't. I started getting tested just before one of the first attempts at writing *Perestroika*. *Millennium* was already done. I think that then—it sounds like ancient history now—whether or not you should get tested was still controversial. AZT hadn't yet been approved; there weren't any good treatment options for opportunistic infections either. So why bother getting tested? All you were doing was providing information for the government to use to put you in a concentration camp.

PP: What were your results?

TK: I'm negative. I had a long discussion with Stephen [Spinella; the actor who plays Prior] when he was interviewed by the *New York Times* about the politics of saying or not saying when he was asked [Spinella was negative]. It's a complicated issue, but I think it's probably useful for people who are seropositive who go to see the play to know that it is written by someone who isn't.

PP: You mentioned in an earlier interview that you were a bit promiscuous in your early sexual experimentation. I think you said you'd gone to bathhouses. Did this cause apprehension when you were tested?

TK: Did I go to bathhouses? I went a couple of times. I'm incredibly shy and I've never been turned on by sex—or even nudity—out in the open. I'm embarrassed by it. The word "promiscuous" I have problems with. But I certainly have been sexually active for a good part of my life, and I've had many partners.

PP: Why are you uncomfortable with the word "promiscuous"?

TK: I don't know. Probably because it has that quality of judgment, that *Scarlet Letter* sense. But I really look back on the days when one could meet a lot of different people—you can still do it— and I think there was something wonderful about it. And I enjoyed it. Apart from the fun I had, I met an outrageous variety of people. Sex is a great leveller. You meet people in an intimate and complicated way that you wouldn't be able to do on the street. I had to write a piece about "Sex In The Time of the Plague" recently for *Esquire* and my first take was, "Everybody should go out and have as much sex as they can get." And then I read about the San Francisco study showing a sharp increase in HIV rates among young gay men. And so I reconsidered my position. How much do you want to know about this?

PP: I'm curious about your sexual history and how it shaped your work, particularly the process of going through testing.

TK: I've been tested several times, and every time I do it I think, "Oh, God, this is it. I did something unsafe somewhere along the line." The first time, I was still with my lover of five years and we'd been completely monogamous. Then I broke up with him and started going around again and my doctor said "You know, you've got the gold standard now."—I'd tested negative and I had a high T-cell count, but it seemed he was talking about currency devaluation—"you really want to think about preserving this." While I'd love to preserve it, I'd also like not to spend the rest of my life not doing anything. And I'm an immensely oral person. I had a long conversation with a group of friends, all serious people, about kissing. Because we didn't know—I guess we still don't completely know—whether it's safer sex. But we thought, "How could you live without it?"

PP: You mean deep tongue kissing?

TK: Yeah. Kissing. I've made out with guys that I've known were HIV+. And had sex with them. And I'm still negative. At least, I think I am. But I do think sex is incredibly important, part of what we are. And I don't think we should let a health issue dictate ... Oh, it's so complicated. I do think people should preserve their health and take care of themselves whether they're seropositive or seronegative. But on the other hand, people shouldn't have to be ...

PP: Hobbled?

TK: Well, we *are* hobbled. There are things people should not do. Many of us miss the taste of cum. But we've got to remain sane about it.

PP: You're saying that deep-kissing someone who is HIV+ is okay?

TK: Well, what I'm saying is, I think it's okay enough to do it. I'll let you know if I'm wrong.

PP: Were you scared or frightened while waiting for your results?

TK: Oh, yeah. Although I've not done anything I consider unsafe in all these years. But there's always the fear and rumours going around about people seroconverting who have never done anything unsafe at all.

PP: Do you feel any guilt about your HIV+ friends?

TK: Sure, I feel guilt. I try to be sensitive about it. I don't go calling up positive friends and crow about my status. And I think there is a tendency among some gay men to turn it into a badge of physical and spiritual superiority in the way that they turn a gym body into that, because white gay men tend to be very status-oriented about a lot of that stuff. And that's particularly repugnant.

PP: How do you handle it, then?

TK: You keep it very clear that you've been spared by accident. I'm thirty-seven years old and this is a very hard world to survive in. But people do survive. I mean, it's really like Holocaust survivors have to think of it. There is a fantasy that a lot of survivors have that they survived because of some clever thing that they did, some way that they outwitted death. But in point of fact, they were just lucky. And luck is this blind thing that flies around and hits some people and doesn't hit others.

PP: Since you brought this up, I wanted to ask you about the Holocaust parallel with AIDS. I know it's a complex issue, but it's worth talking about.

TK: I firmly believe in using the Holocaust model, promiscuously. I think we should be very liberal with likening people to Nazis. I wrote a play about this [*Bright Room Called Day*]. I think that the worst thing you can do to any historical event is to turn it into some kind of magic moment that happened for a metaphysical reason that doesn't have anything to do with the materialist conditions of history. The Holocaust has become the paradigm for human evil, and then we turn and say there was nothing like it before in history and nothing will be like it in the future. For the people who went through it, it's understandable to say that. But it's also a terrible mistake. Milosevic is a Nazi and Ronald Reagan is a Nazi. This is not to say that Reagan walks around in a black uniform. But he cynically manipulated an issue and allowed the situation to become more dangerous. I think the indifference the West has shown to AIDS in developing countries is genocidal and I wonder how many gay men, who have been so wonderful in responding to men in our own community, will continue to worry about it when, as I hope will happen, medical advances make it into a maintenance illness or get rid of it. There will still be an economics of infection and prevention in other parts of the world. And will we still care?

PP: Is it possible to say how being negative affected the writing of the play? Would the play be different if you'd tested HIV+?

TK: I'm sure it would have had a profound effect on me and consequently on my work. I just finished interviewing a lot of HIV+ people for *Vanity Fair*, and every single one of them said that before they'd gotten the results they didn't know how they were going to handle it and that the way they did only evolved after some time had passed. I'm sure that would be true of me, too.

PP: Within this context, it's intriguing to look at Prior and how he copes with his situation. Was it clear from the beginning of the writing that Prior would not die?

TK: I knew that Roy was going to die. The play was designed to culminate in a certain way with Roy's death, but the main person with AIDS was Prior. And the point is that people *do* survive. It's seriously under-represented. You don't want to be pie-in-the-sky about it, but there can be years and years of very productive life. And I thought there was an incredible unwillingness to show that. That it was a widespread form of delectation among those who are not immune-compromised to show over and over again people dying these terrible deaths because it makes you cry. Unfortunately, it's considered one of the hallmarks of success in theatre or film if you can make the audience break down at the end. And I think that's disgusting.

It's terribly important that *Perestroika* ends with an epilogue, five years into the future, and that Prior is still alive. He's having a hard time. He's not necessarily going to be alive a lot longer. And yet he *could* be. It doesn't end with that. And some people are pissed off at that.

PP: Why?

TK: Although the literature of AIDS has gotten more sophisticated, there's still the expectation that AIDS equals death at the end. Which is why I love the responses that audiences have at the end of *Millennium*. Because it's possible that Prior is dead at the end, but it's clearly not a scene that allows you to sit there and weep over somebody quietly expiring in a hospital bed. It's this wild event. And I think people really know he hasn't died. But I have had people come up to me afterward and say, "He didn't die at the end. Is that realistic?" They felt cheated of their deathbed scene.

PP: Have PWAs accused you of denial?

TK: No. But part of the struggle Prior goes through in *Perestroika* is specifically over this issue. I know I said I wasn't going to lecture anybody, but I will say this: In my experience with this as with other illnesses, it does make a difference how you live your life. Do you take care of yourself? Do you actively, aggressively seek out good medical attention? Do you question your doctor? And it's terribly hard to do those things. You have to resist both the notion that you can absolutely control this through will—which isn't true and only makes some people feel like they've failed when they've gotten sick—and the idea that it's a death sentence that will be carried out in a couple of months. In *Perestroika* I wanted to represent somebody having an immensely difficult time getting himself to do those things. One of the things I like about Prior is that he's someone who doesn't see himself as a strong person. He sees himself as a fragile queen who isn't going to be able to bear up under all the horror and abandonment. And he finds himself to be a tremendously strong person with great courage, which has been very true to my own experience in a lot of people.

PP: What's also intriguing to me about Prior is the idea that he's expected to be some kind of prophet. But he refuses that role, doesn't he? What does this mean?

TK: It's very complicated, and it's part of what my struggle over the rewrites of *Perestroika* have been about—exactly how clear I want to make this. I find that when I spell out the various possibilities of the meaning of it, it makes the play lose what is shaggy and strange, which is what I like. What Prior is refusing is a very specific message and a very specific part of himself that he needs to refuse in order to make his decision: not just *to survive* but that *he wants* to survive. I think these are very different things. I think that if it was anybody's decision to live, most people would decide that they would want to. But when you don't have the choice, then to make the decision that you *would like* to live is sometimes very difficult. Because sometimes death—for the planet, in a certain sense—has become an attractive option. What I'm trying to explore in Prior is one of the great mysteries. It's hard to explain without sounding sentimental, but this is why human beings survive things that seem so unendurable. It's not survivalism. It's not "fuck everybody else, I'm going to stay alive." It's the question of the will to live: is it just biology? Is it just fear? Is it an addiction (which is what Prior calls it at one point)? Even when there is clearly no joy left in life, why is it that we won't surrender? And that's what *Perestroika* is all about, what Prior's struggle with the angels is all about. What they're offering him is what all religion offers—the solace of what comes after.

PP: And that's opposed to change, isn't it? The angels are reactionary; they demand paralysis.

TK: Yes. They want paralysis, illness, an end to change and progress. The Angel of History wants to go back and restore what has been destroyed. But the winds of time are inevitably blowing her forward.

PP: That's what I think gives the play such hope: the embrace of change, even in someone unexpected, like the character of the

Mormon mother. What about the changes in your own personal life? How did you manage those? Say, in your search for sex, love, and affection?

TK: I have a tremendously strong mating and domesticating impulse. From the age of twenty-one, when I had my first sexual encounter, I began meeting guys and having sex, but I was thinking, "Oh, God, it's so empty." I'd had sex with three people and I was already experiencing this John Rechy-thing about it all being so meaningless. What I wanted was to have a boyfriend. I wanted to be in love. And I still do. It's very hard for me to live alone, and I wanted to have somebody at home. I'd read all the novels in which there were these guys in their great apartments with their cute lovers. It's a tremendously potent fantasy.

PP: In *Angels* you deal with the insufficiency of love, the abandonment of Prior by Louis. How realistic is that?

TK: I think what Louis does is shocking. Realistic? Well, yes, I know two people who walked out on people who were sick. They weren't like Louis—they were actually kind of trashy. I've seen the entire spectrum of behaviour in terms of people taking care of people. I've seen people who are just spectacular, incredibly great about it; some who were not so great but who hung in there to the best of their powers; and I've seen people who were there in name only. That's another thing I felt was missing from representations of the health crisis: how tremendously hard it is for people to take care of other people. Some have a genius for it; others don't. It seems to me that one of the ironies of history is that during the age of Reagan while we were being told that incredible selfishness was the key to all truth and goodness, many people who had not been raised in the art of self-sacrifice were being asked to make incredible sacrifices and to overcome their natural tendency to run away from calamity. And Louis was my way of dealing with that. Representing those things is one of the duties of drama. It's what Goethe said about *Young Werther*: you write about it so you don't do it. Louis is not some shit. He isn't oblivious to the consequences of his actions. He knows he's walking from the frying pan into the fire, and in *Perestroika* you know the depths of his guilt. He knows he's made a mistake. And he knows how far he wants to go to pay for it in his own crazy way.

PP: What you've put your finger on is the awesome power of AIDS to transform us.

TK: Yes, I believe that.

PP: Did taking care of friends with AIDS affect the rewriting of *Perestroika*?

TK: It's made it harder. I'll be completely honest with you. The process of rewriting *Perestroika* is so completely and totally overwhelmed by the need to follow *Millennium* that almost any other consideration is nearly obliterated by it. I set myself up. I didn't know that *Millennium* was going to succeed to the extent that it did. But the success of *Millennium* has become a terrible obstacle that has to be overcome. I'm fighting against that and the expectations it raises more than anything else.

Millennium ends with wild fantasy. You don't know if that's the angel of death or the angel of deliverance, but it's gorgeous and it's fun. But *Perestroika* is about everybody finding their way back to reality, which is disappointing and small and hard. I love it when people say about *Millennium,* "It felt like one hour," but *Perestroika* may feel like five hours. It may be five hours! I hope people are grown up about it.

As for AIDS, I feel a lot angrier than I used to. I was always angry about government indifference and the greed of the big pharmaceutical companies, about the way in which society has responded to the plague—I feel very mad about that. But there is a certain kind of anger toward God that has come into *Perestroika* more and more because there are people I have lost, or am perhaps in the process of losing, and I really don't want to let go of them. I've discovered an incredible rage in myself that's worked its way in. *Perestroika* is an uglier, angrier play.

PP: And that rage is directed toward both the government and toward God?

TK: Well, the government is always doing something that makes one angry. I'm not a gay man who got politicized because of a health crisis. The government is always appalling. As much as I despised the Republicans, even I was shocked by the response to AIDS by Reagan and Bush. I couldn't believe that someone as conscious of PR as Reagan could be so blind as to what history is going to make of the way he behaved.

PP: But Reagan was obtuse about history. He said he didn't care because he wasn't going to be around to read it anyway.

TK: Yeah, but he also thought he could rewrite it. I really was astonished in the '80s at the extent to which people believed—and it wasn't only Reagan, though he's culpable because he was elected to be a leader—the way in which society as a whole believed for a long time—believed that we deserved to die because we had sex with each other. This may be changing now, though I don't really know. I still find the depths of homophobia very frightening.

I thought that after the inauguration—as tacky as that might have been—"Well, now the new order has begun, and Clinton is going to do it. We're going to have moved forward a decade in two months. Clinton will be queer-positive and the whole country will have to change." I look back on that now and wonder what I was thinking?

PP: It makes you feel naive?

TK: It does. And there are all these unpleasant surprises like Sam Nunn turning into Jesse Helms. What happened to that guy? I never liked him all that much, but he turned into a raving nutbag.

PP: But the military issue isn't a question of life and death like AIDS.

TK: I don't agree. I believe that one of the major lessons in discrimination today is what Louis says in *Millennium*, "When the shit hits the fan, you realize just how much tolerance is worth." To be tolerated is worth nothing. Because if you're merely tolerated and you get in trouble, you're going to die. Only by having the status of a full citizen, guaranteed by law, are you protected.

PP: And that applies both to the Holocaust and to AIDS?

TK: Yes. The argument is right out of Hannah Arendt. The German Jews made a very big mistake when they accepted a status that was less than German. If you're going to be given a choice between being a pariah and a parvenu, be a pariah because the parvenus are easily dispensed with.

PP: What do you think of Clinton's response to AIDS?

TK: Has there been one? He's given us more money. It's less than he promised but it's something. We now have an AIDS—one would hesitate to call her a Czar—I don't know exactly what Kristine Gebbie is. I think Larry Kramer is absolutely right when he says that Clinton's been incredibly bad about appointments and that it's all been too sluggish. I think Clinton's doing what Bush and Reagan did to this extent: I think he's horsetrading with the issue. I think he's not really willing to make it a big deal to start with because he was trying to get the budget through. But, of course, time is of the essence here. And that infuriates me. Is the federal government going to get behind serious safer-sex education? Or can we expect nothing more than the same malignant dicking around that goes on all the time in Congress?

PP: At this point do you think that Clinton is as culpable as Reagan and Bush?

TK: Oh, no. It's hard to give him the time he deserves because he's not a very appealing person, he's too Machiavellian. And we've been deprived for so long—we being the entire populace except for rich, straight, white men—of any expectation of decency from the federal government, so, of course, we're very impatient now. And we have a right to be, and we ought to be, or we'll let Clinton off the hook. He's only going to be dragged into this issue kicking and screaming. I don't think he's an evil man like Bush, but I think he's a rather spineless one.

PP: What's frightening is what is going to happen when the shit hits the fan in the coming decade. It could get uglier.

TK: That's of course scary. I love the way that universal health care—the issue Clinton won on—has now become a way of saving the government money on health care, which is very frightening in terms of AIDS.

PP: Isn't that the most difficult thing about change? Whether you're talking about government or the play or speaking personally. That accommodation to loss?

TK: When I first started writing the second play, I wanted to call it *Perestroika* because I had this wild-eyed notion that Gorbachev was going to make the world a different place and bring about the advent of democratic socialism, which is what makes the most amount of sense to me. And then, of course, things began to go from good to bad to really awful in the former Soviet bloc. There were times I thought I should change the title of the play now because perestroika has not fulfilled its promise.

But actually in its way it has. In one of the clearer moments in his book Gorbachev says that our job is simply to make change irreversible. I believe that change is terribly hard, but I don't believe that it's impossible, and that's the hope in *Perestroika*. And I believe that the worst thing ever is to try and reverse the course of progress, because reaching back to a fantasy past is the hallmark of Reaganism, and the idea of containing change is the ideology of Roy Cohn. And the defeat of these is what we're committed to right now.

PP: Do your characters conquer loss?

TK: They face it. You can't conquer loss. You lose. To suggest otherwise would be to suggest a fantasy. The characters do fantasize to a certain extent: Harper has a speech at the end of *Perestroika* in which she imagines that there is some way in which the losses of the world are working toward some other kind of gain so that, as she says, they're not lost forever. I don't believe that, as human beings, we can do anything other than struggle to face loss with grace, as Harper says, as much as we can.

PP: And the ultimate loss is death.

TK: Yes. And life is about losing. Things are taken from you. People are taken from you. You just have to face it. And let go. Which is the gesture of losing. You have to allow yourself to let go and it's complicated. Because you always run the danger of becoming passive in the face of the agents of loss that should have been resisted, and you don't want to end up doing that, either.

Flying in
Different Directions

by Bent Holm

Henning Olesen as Roy Cohn in Aarhus Teater's
production of *Engle i Amerika*. Photo © Jan Jul.

Flying in Different Directions: American Angels in Denmark

by Bent Holm
translated by Per Brask

Angels in America was produced in Denmark in two versions in the Spring of 1995. The provincial stage, Aarhus Teater, presented Part One, and the national theatre, Det Kongelige Teater, Parts One and Two; on a number of occasions both parts were presented in one, eight-hour performance.

Moving a play to a cultural context so different from its original implies a series of difficulties which can be neglected or faced. In connection with *Angels in America*, the key word is "controversy," but in a Nordic context what is controversial is found in dimensions other than those most overtly implied by the play.[1] A number of issues concerning Danish conditions in general will probably clarify what the discussion refers to.

As for the religious dimension, the reality is that sects such as the Mormons hardly exist. Rather, they appear to be bizarre phenomena for most people. Churches/religions, such as Catholics or Jews, are minority phenomena without, for example, any political importance. The Lutheran state church has no real power. Mentally, people are secularized without a common set of spiritual concepts, symbols or images.[2] The attitude towards religion is generally awkward compared, for example, to the attitude towards sex. Being

BENT HOLM, Dr. phil. in Dramaturgy, has produced a substantial body of work, including articles and books on Holberg, Dario Fo and Commedia Dell'arte. He has also worked extensively as a production dramaturge and a translator.

a uni-ethnic country, (vulgar) racism is directed towards marginal (Muslim) minority groups of immigrants and refugees.

Public morality—sexual, political, etc.—is also rather relaxed and tolerant, with little hysteria or Puritanism. It is an unwritten law, for example, that politicians' private, sexual lives are taboo for the press. If a scandal occurs, it exposes the reporter, not the "sinner." This situation is beginning to change, however, and we can now foresee American conditions. The number of political scandals of any importance is rather low. There is no serious tradition for corruption or dirty tricks. The right-wing government of the '80s definitely did flirt with Reaganism and Thatcherism. A certain yuppie life-style became fashionable but without the element of the marked cold-warriors' come-back. The cold war, McCarthyism, etc., are distant, rather forgotten phenomena, at least for the younger generations. Nevertheless, America's cultural influence (through movies, television, life styles, etc.) is enormous. Homosexuality is an issue of little or no controversy, though attitudes naturally vary between the cities and other parts of the country; Denmark has one of the world's most liberal legislations. For instance, in 1989, as a result of four years of investigation by a government commission into the condition of homosexuals in society, Parliament passed a law about registered partnership. Plays about AIDS, such as William Hoffmann's As Is and Larry Kramer's The Normal Heart, were presented in 1986, one year after their New York premieres. Danish playwrights also deal with these topics in theatre, television and radio. Of course the fear of AIDS is as serious as elsewhere but the openness in the official campaigns has been remarked on internationally.

Among God, politics, and sex, then, perhaps the most mysterious remains God, in the sense that more crucial, existential/ "mythological" themes lack a language, a field of reference. Of course physical degradation and death, in the shape of AIDS, make the resulting emptiness painfully present and the other issues become secondary because they are not half as traumatic. In short, the radical confrontation with ultimate confusion and destruction becomes the powerful core of the play in this context, its fundamental interfusion of mind and body. On the other hand, its realistic or documentary aspects, including issues of gayness, become less central because they are less controversial.[3] The "Gay Fantasia" angle supplies the conflicts, dilemmas and perplexities with an extra dimension of, perhaps, allegorical nature.

The play's musical structure is determined by the dissolution of the body intermingled with consciences and minds. The dissolution of the personality—or the play's momentous dive underneath the human surface—might suggest that one mind has a kind of priority, and that it consists of three subjects, simplified drastically as follows: Joe Pitt, marked strongly by morality; Louis Ironson, the ironic, marked by intellect and Prior, marked, possibly, by lust.[4] In any case their spiritual universes converge in the mind of Prior, the one whose church doesn't "believe in Mormons" (act 1, scene 7). He is not religious but nevertheless hears the Hebrew (act 3, scene 3), sees the burning book with the Aleph (act 3, scene 3) and the angel, and becomes the prophet (act 3, scene 8). Even if it is the Mormon Joe who identifies with the Old Testament tale about Jacob's wrestling with the angel, (act 2, scene 2), it is Prior who fulfils it in Part Two (act 5, scene 1). This one mind communicates with, among others, Harper's mind, just as Roy has his own, personal, sub- or superhuman contacts. Perhaps Belize has the clearest view and the least angelic relationship. And this is only perhaps because if one considers the distribution of roles among actors this proposed system collapses; another system interferes. As Tony Kushner says in the *Note about the Staging* in Part Two, "A membrane has broken; there is disarray and debris." The acceleration of traffic through the broken membrane seems to be the primary motor in the theatrical engine. It might seem that the concept of reality changes in the Epilogue, Part Two: Prior speaks "to the audience;" we are back again in a kind reality that has an existence in itself, marked by *breaking the illusion*. The movement from "collective dream," "stream of consciousness" (or whatever insufficient term could be chosen) to the exterior world, is a sort of wake-up call to the theatre's "reality!"

Though a director in a Danish context would not operate in a homophobic post-McCarthyistic, puritan-hypocritical culture, there are still abundant dimensions on which to focus. Looking for controversy here demands other accents and balances.

The Aarhus Theatre is the regional theatre in the second biggest Danish town. It has two larger stages and two smaller ones. In general, the biggest stage, with 700 seats, presents a repertoire intended for a broad audience. The larger of the two smaller theatres, with 270 seats, presents a less conventional repertoire intended for younger generations. It was on this stage that *Angels in America* was produced in order to reach a young audience. The director was the Swedish theatre, film and television director, Johan Bergenstråhle, born 1935. In the 1980s, he directed a TV series on the life of Strindberg with Tommy Berggreen. Most of his productions have been produced at Stockholm's Stadsteater (City Theatre of Stockholm). His most controversial production at the Aarhus Theatre was Fassbinder's *The Burning City* in 1983. Johan Bergenstråhle died on August 23, 1995, making *Angels in America* his last theatre production.

Aarhus Theatre presented Part One, premiering February 10, 1995,[5] without changing or cutting any part of the text. A thorough "who's who," combined with documentation/information about Mormons, and others, was published in the program to diminish the problems of context. The production was produced with due attention to Tony Kushner's *Note About the Staging:* "The play benefits from a pared-down style of presentation, with minimal scenery and scene shifts done rapidly (no blackouts!) employing the cast as well as stage-hands, which makes for an actor-driven event, as this must be."

The stage in Aarhus was a rhombic platform becoming narrower towards the back, with two "wings" on the sides and steps at the front. It was painted in stone-like greenish nuances. On each side was a sink and no other indications of place. The audience was seated slightly amphitheatrically in the auditorium, which is sloped, and on either side of the platform halfway turned towards the stage. Chairs placed in front of the audience were occasionally used by the actors when not in a scene. This configuration meant that the conventional borderline between stage and auditorium was softly moderated. Part of the action could take place in the auditorium, as in the Antarctic scene (act 3, scene 4) when Harper escaped to the rear of the auditorium and from there conversed with Mr. Lies. The distribution of parts among the actors was in complete accordance with the author's directions, including women playing male parts. The title of each act was written with chalk on the black back wall as a kind of graffiti.

The transitions were all smooth and flexible, achieved by the actors assisted by four extras dressed elegantly in black. This created a never-ending musical rhythm, having most of the *dramatis personae* stay on or near the stage either as witnesses to the action commenting through their (non-) presence, or as spectators. For instance, after Harper's trip to Antarctica she crouches on the stage floor in her polar outfit and stays there during the Bronx scene (act 3, scene 5) as part of a visual construction that includes the homeless woman and Hannah who has lost her way. She stays through the following scene with Joe and Roy, the final seduction attempt, and during the scene with Ethel Rosenberg, Prior one and Prior two, while she and Prior "wake up" during Joe's and Louis's kiss in scene 8—a meeting which does not take place "in the park on a bench" but on the bare stage. The action proceeds smoothly into the final visit of the angel to Prior, who is standing wrapped up in a sheet (referring to his bed which we saw earlier).

Of course such connections suggested by the staging were thematically loaded or infected. One typical example, which proves to involve themes of cleanliness, purity, purification, is introduced in the transition from scene 1, the burial, where the coffin ends up being carried out while Roy's desk is carried in. At the same time Louis and Prior are at the front of the stage as Roy and Joe enter having fun with each other, producing an atmosphere of schoolmates teasing or a father-son relationship. This serves to weave scene 1 and scene 2 together. Roy offers sandwiches to Joe and then *throws* one to him. The image of the servant/underdog is clear, even if it all happens in a merry and friendly atmosphere. Joe then unfolds his white handkerchief and carefully picks up the sandwich from the ground, places it in the cloth and puts it back on the dish, i.e., cleans up the little mess. This reaction immediately reveals Joe's concern for cleanliness and his efforts to protect himself from impurity as well as his sub-status, and Roy's dynamic, extroverted nature, energy and superiority. The impression is reinforced by Joe assisting Roy in adjusting his tie, in order to build up his perfect image. These small gestures are based on hints implicit in the text which in the dramatic situation deepen the relationships. During Harper's monologue, which follows, about the ozone-layer (scene 3: "she speaks to the audience") played on the empty stage, Joe is seen in the background with an umbrella, protecting himself. He comes back "home," changes clothes and washes his hands, preparing to face Harper. These details are essential for developing Joe's character and his story. In scene 6 in the men's room, Joe frenetically supplies the unhappy Louis with metres of toilet paper to dry his tears. As the dissolution of Joe's "normal" personality is becoming apparent (and the dramatic universe as a whole is corrupting and dissolving), it is accompanied theatrically by an increasing invasion of the stage by waste and garbage; the scrap becomes visible. In act 2, scene 5, the flowers Belize brings for Prior in the hospital eventually end up on the floor where they are left scattered till the end of the show. Later on, when Joe meets Louis outside the Court building (act 2, scene 7)—a location in this production indicated only by the dialogue—he is frantically devouring hot dogs and cokes. When Louis gets sick of the junk food, Joe offers him his handkerchief to clean his mouth; after he uses it, he returns it to Joe who hesitates for a moment, then uses it on his own mouth, and drops it on the ground/stage floor (see the above mentioned use of handkerchief and toilet paper for cleaning up and helping the unhappy). All Joe's waste is left on the stage while, desperately roaring, he begins to undress. He now completely lacks balance. Joe says "what a thing it would be ... if overnight everything you owe anything to, justice or love, had really gone away. Free. It would be ... heartless terror. Yes. Terrible, and ... Very great. *To shed your skin*, every old skin, one by one and then walk away, unencumbered, into the morning." Clearly a kind of birth is taking place. Joe is almost naked and then when Prior helps him dress in a rather confused way, some of his garments are inside-out. This is a crucial turning point, especially when accompanied by the increasingly littered stage, which is now strewn with sausages, paper, coke cans. After Louis's conversation with Belize about democracy and racism (act 3, scene 3), snow begins to fall as a relief. The garbage theme reaches a climax when, in scene 5, three mobile, visible wind machines are activated by the extras and actually blow waste onto the stage. The junk food from act 2 is still there and in the scene with Hannah and the homeless woman, the latter picks up a sausage and begins to eat it. The wind machines are activated again when, in scene 6, Roy almost assaults Joe in a long kiss just before Joe leaves and Ethel arrives. After the kiss Joe rushes out, evidently sick. Joe's concern with litter, which is seen when food was thrown to him by Roy at the beginning and he picked it up in his handkerchief, is pursued to a complex climax in cascades of waste. The physical transformation of the (inner) stage is almost complete, and, in addition, the alchemists (act 3, scene 7) spread palm and rose leaves on the floor.

As already noted, one leading principle of this production was the accentuation of the characters' relationships by a special emphasis on physical aspects—the body as a metaphor. A result of this was that the verbal dimension—the intellectual, sophisticated wit—was toned down, as was the detailed description of the external world. Thus the priority was moved from exterior and intellectual drama to interior and physical drama. Some examples: the relationship between Harper and Joe is concretely, physically desperate. As they get closer, as for example in Act 1, Scene 5, when she offers "to give a blowjob ... You want to try? ... Mormons can give blowjobs," they are lying on the floor and she is clinging to him in a sort of pathetic *pietá*; when Roy has been examined by the doctor (act 1, scene 9) he enters nude and dresses during the following dialogue, building up his macho personality and revealing his aggressive nature in Humphrey Bogart-like grimaces; when Belize visits Prior (act 2, scene 5) he happily plants his flowers at Prior's nude genitals and gives an intimate "gentle massage" with the "voodoo cream from the botanical round the block"[6] on his inner thighs; the already mentioned act 2, scene 7, where Joe changes skin/clothes; Harper changes clothes from her eternal night-gown to a dress when she has decided to leave Joe (act 2, scene 9); later in the same scene Joe vomits blood in his handkerchief (note the paragraph above about the cleanness theme—just as in act 2, scene 1 we saw blood when Prior "shits himself"). There is evident erotic tension between Harper and Mr. Lies (act 3, scene 4). Perhaps the most significant example of all, since it supplies the scene with a new dimension, is the Louis-Belize dialogue (act 3, scene 3) about democracy and racism, which is presumed to take place "in a coffee shop." In this production this scene was presented on the empty stage with no chairs, no coffee. In the background Prior is seen wandering, dressed in a white hospital dress drawing his drop, a kind of modern and secular *via crucis* in a state of despair. From time to time he bursts into song, namely "Liebestod" from *Tristan und Isolde*. This theme was already touched upon by his drag entry in his and Harper's common dream and hallucination scene (act 1, scene 7) where he is introduced by a Maria Callas aria from *Madame Butterfly*. Prior's singing alternates with Louis's intellectual tirades, and supplies them with a painful resonance. Furthermore, the text of this scene, as such, gives very little meaning in a Danish context (see above) and may seem somewhat rhetorical. However, the scene presented as it was became one of the strongest in the play by the use of contrast and the concretization of Louis's dilemma.

From these explorations in the non-verbal stratums it may have become clear that the interpretation was not primarily comedic. The audience did not laugh unrestrainedly. The basic tone was not brilliantly sarcastic, but rather serious, the characters were under pressure. Though the light wit, especially between Prior and Belize, was brilliant, its context was still rather dark. The only character who does not master the ironic tone is Joe. And he sets the tone for this production. Audience empathy was mainly with his dilemma(s), his conflict received high priority. This does not mean he was drawn as a sad and tense character. He was presented as a man who tried to be merry and kind and whose reactions when they went out of control easily slipped to grotesque euphoria.

A complaint might be that supernatural, magic moments were somewhat toned down or not sufficiently elaborated, especially considering the fact that, for a Danish audience, such a dimension has no evident significance in itself.[7] That is true, for example, with the ghost scenes. Further, the "Shakespearean" lack of visual indication of place implied a demand for stringent ways of operating all levels and aspects of the play's musicality. This was not always one hundred percent honoured; orientation was lost in ways that did not support the story. However, as to the play being controversial, the production coped with the previously mentioned difficulties confronted when producing the play in Denmark by moving its emphasis to a very direct elaboration of the traumatic conflict and dilemmas. This was done, for example, by using the body as a metaphor, and it seems to have succeeded, in spite of the complications involved in transplanting the play to different soil.

The production was especially addressed to a young generation, and reached them to an overwhelming degree. I have chosen four important newspapers to give a broad impression of the production's reception in the press: the two grand old morning papers, one of them more central/social-democratic oriented, *Politiken* (often considered trend-setting in its theatre reviews), and one more conservative, *Berlingske Tidende*; and the two smaller, more elite ones, again one more to the left, *Information*, and one more to the right, *Weekendavisen* (published once a week). In order to elucidate my introductory remarks, I have chosen to consider the following important elements in the reviews: opinions expressed on the play, its themes, the (leading) characters, and the staging on a political, a psychological/sexual, and a religious level; though these issues were not always attended to by the reviewers.

Bettina Heltberg (middle generation) from *Politiken* says that "It is a brilliant text, full of wit and psychology" (February 12, 1995). She defines the main theme as "the radical dream of liberation of the oppressed" according to Martin Luther King's "famous words to the people: I have a dream," and finds, with respect to the background of AIDS ("a cultural metaphor") and the figure of Roy Cohn "one of the most important 'national themes' ... the personal lie as instrument for survival in society." Another "national theme" presented is "the claim of the strong to the realm." As "Tony Kushner's coup consists of placing oppression and self-oppression in a framework of political and cultural backlash," Roy Cohn becomes one of the most interesting characters. He is defined as "a villain" and "a victim of non-liberty," but foremost "a morbid American father figure." A central scene is Joe's breakdown and change in act 2, scene 7, "like a primal cry of sorrow, pain, convulsive crying and terror, a violent sexual birth accompanied by a physical change of skin," whereas Louis's and Prior's love-story, she suggests, is understated, even if Prior is being "the one in whom all the others perhaps are born as hallucinations or fever visions." The staging is criticized for starting in too "normal" a register, "then gradually discovering that we have to go further down and out. Downwards and home. Finally we arrive." The political perspective is seen as an American one, the psychological/sexual perspective as commonly valid, and, as for the religious perspective, she involves Christ's Sermon for a discussion of the question of whether suffering and minority themes and points of view have a universal value in general terms. In short, the play is brilliant, the staging only partly successful, finally the production's level of "psychological persuasion" did not work because it did not succeed in bringing together the play's themes.

The critic of *Berlingske Tidende*, Me Lund (younger generation) had promoted the play in the press after its London production, stating that "once every ten years a trend-setting, renewing drama emerges" and that *Angels in America* was that drama. She describes *Angels in America* as "gay drama and universal drama in one ... under the headline 'what to do with our lives in a world without permanent values?'" As for the religious theme, the angelic dimension, she states that "God's own country is crowded with angels. Fallen angels. Angels who have lost their orientation after God

died—or at least disappeared." The main significance is clearly seen
as the moral-existential theme. Thus the play is immediately intelli-
gible. But the staging lacks the emotional quality of the text "due to
a fundamentally wrong choice made by the director. Fearing to
exaggerate a gay point of view he has toned it down … Joe's fight for
getting out of the closet is given far too much as is his conflict with
the father figure Roy Cohn … it's wrong from the beginning: Why is
the rabbi played by a woman …? Is there a connection between the
four parts the actress presents …? Apparently not …. It is difficult to
find a coherent idea behind these decisions,[8] just as it is difficult to
find out with whom the production sides. It ought not to have been
all that difficult. It ought to have sided with the whole text, with
both couples of angels." One almost gets the impression that the
critic had expected something different—perhaps something closer
to the London production? She considers the play an absolute mas-
terpiece but this staging unsuccessful.

On February 13, *Information* published a review by Erik Thygesen
(middle generation), giving a large and profound introduction to the
historical-political background. Thygesen remarks that he is not
sure that the play has been appropriately promoted "as the great,
definitive dramatic production about the AIDS wave," because the
play "is about so many other things. It is a condemnation of America
so clamorous that one might wonder … why the American embassy
has not arranged anti-angel demonstrations against Aarhus Teater."
"The play is written with a film-like quality, but even that is less
newsworthy than it was once." For Thygesen, Cohn provides an
entry to the play. After a description of his merits Thygesen
concludes, "how strange suddenly to face this disgusting person.
And what a personal challenge to be put in a position where, if the
play is to work at all, you necessarily must feel for and with this
monster.… Cohn was definitely a subordinate character, but he was
an excellent choice as a focal character if you, like Tony Kushner, see
a connection between the AIDS-epidemic and Reagan's political
dominance in the USA of the '80s." As Roy is the representative of
the "USA as the super-power of lies and hypocrisy," Joe personifies
another important, traumatic American theme: the loss of
innocence. Thirdly comes Prior. He is an angel among the other,
more symbolic or theoretical, Mormon and avenging angels. "He
presents the hope. Even if he dies of the disease, he is the hope. An
amazing, but nevertheless credible character."[9] The staging is de-

scribed in terms of "an amazingly precise, amazingly small story. The manuscript tends towards large gestures. Except for the *grande finale*, the director has chosen intimate theatrical devices. And they work." Thus Thygesen sees it as a play about a specific time and place and, as such, worthwhile interrogating. The play is good, the staging excellent.

Jens Kistrup (older generation) in *Weekendavisen* (February 17th) also interrogates the text, though from a different point of view, but even he maintains the American background. Kistrup defines it as a very moral play which makes very difficult demands on its characters as well as on the entire American society, "just as difficult—and as impossible—as the demands Gregers Werle made to Hjalmar Ekdal in *The Wild Duck*. We know the disastrous result." Those demands—"say what you mean! Confess who you are, sexually and politically! Avoid dissimulation and hypocrisy!"—Imply that "everybody is put under moral watch and control. A terrifying thought! ... Almost everything is seen through the lens of morality and sexuality which locks the play in a kind of monomaniacal stubbornness which can become a problem for the theatre as well as the audience." The primary theme is defined as gay love, but the play has many themes, and its seductive effect depends on the way they interact with each other, at the same time strengthening and weakening the totality and the details, portraying "USA as a society in which all hope, all faith, all love seem to be consumed. In spite of the angel which at the very end descends from the heavens (the borders) as a messenger without a message."[10] Roy and Joe are mentioned as central characters. "And I think Johan Bergenstraahle's staging has done the right thing in understating the (homo)sexual theme and underlining the consequences of suppression and hypocrisy." Kistrup problematizes the play, giving voice to a (perhaps "European?") skepticism towards its presumed longing for straightforwardness, innocence. He observes from a position of distance, of non-identification, and maybe indirectly he happens to reveal a congruency between Joe's dilemma and the play's, concerning the theme of purity. Kistrup considers the production much better than the play.

   None of the critics go into noteworthy discussions about the form and structure of the play, and consequently do not deal with how these affect its meaning. They focus on political and moral aspects,

Above: Henning Olesen as Roy Cohn
in Aarhus Teater's production of
Engle i Amerika.
Right: Torben Jensen as Roy Cohn in
Det Kongelige Teater's production of
Engle i Amerika.

while the (deeper) layers of conscience, meaning, and reality (i.e., the suggestive, non-verbal dimensions) are hardly touched.

Det Kongelige Teater (The Royal Theatre) is the Danish national theatre with the largest artistic and technical resources. It has two large stages, one for opera and ballet and one for drama, and a small stage for more experimental theatre. The stage for drama has 700 seats. It is a regular proscenium theatre. The repertoire is, by law, well-rounded: national and international, classic and modern—as is the case in Aarhus. The fact that *Angels in America* was performed on the big stage meant that the play was addressed to a broad audience; there was no specific target group. The director was Jan Maagaard who, born in Denmark 1945, has directed plays in Denmark, Germany and Sweden. From 1987–91 he was artistic director of the Klara Scene at Stockholm's Stadsteater (City Theatre of Stockholm). Since 1991 he has been a resident director at Det Kongelige Teater in Copenhagen where he has directed a number of large productions, including *Mourning Becomes Electra* in 1991.

The opening of *Angels in America* was one week after Aarhus's, February 2, 1995.[11] Two weeks later Part Two was presented, and combined with Part One in a number of marathon-performances lasting eight hours each.

The text used by Det Kongelige Teater was the same version as used in the former production, with some modifications. Some of the play's rhetorical character was eliminated, giving the text a tendency towards a normal and realistic dialogue without too many specific American references. Harper's self-reflecting lines were cut, making the character more credible, partly due to different theatrical conventions; so was Joe's description of her unhappy childhood and background (act 2, scene 4), which in Aarhus had the character of a real monologue. The explicit, self-distancing style, drawn from epic rhetorical theatre forms, was slightly modified creating the advantage of a tone familiar from, for example, American movies. The program offered extensive documentation about McCarthyism, Mormonism, AIDS, etc.

The roles were distributed among the actors mainly according to the manuscript, except that Henry, Roy's doctor, was played by a male actor, not by "Hannah," and that the figure of Martin Heller ("Harper") was removed. This left the only cross-gender casting between Rabbi Chemelwitz and Hannah. The performance started with the actress being dressed for the part, a meta-fictional effect that was not continued except in Mr. Lies's entries which were announced by stage-hands dispersing smoke.

The very first thing seen by the audience was a transparent curtain on which the titles were projected and on which were drawn cloud-like spiral lines. The set itself was dominated by a number of brownish monoliths: obelisks with their tops slopingly cut off and silvery patterns on the top surface, suggesting brain or other organic matter. They were moved and combined in different ways and, except for sexual connotations, were mainly drawing the skyline of New York. The tops of the buildings were seen partly "from above"; the sloped cut suggested to the audience an angel's point of view. Changes of location were identified by the use of actual articles such as benches, arm-chairs, tables, lamps, etc., usually in accordance with the stage directions. Harper's and Joe's place was furnished with a floor lamp and furniture, and Louis's and Prior's with a great double bed with a red bed-side lamp (the bed was outfitted with an end piece slightly resembling a coffin). In the scene when Joe and Louis meet outside the court building (act 2, scene 7) an actual hot dog stand was on stage. The hospital was symbolized with a neon sign which read "EMERGENCY." Certain scenes were played in front of a curtain so the variation of location was rather wide, even if it was not a realistic one (indeed, even Utah was constructed by the monoliths). In general, the locations in the split scenes were well distinguished or defined, the staging working more with simultaneity than with inter-mixing. In some scenes the visual effect was rather expressive, for example, in act 1, scene 4, and carried on in scene 6, when Roy attempts a kind of demonic seduction of Joe accompanied by the punishment/intercourse scene between Louis and the man in the park. The background was flaming red, and the bar table behind which Roy stood was illuminated so that his face was lit from beneath suggesting an almost infernal effect, clearly announcing the hellish Roy in Part Two, where, after his death, Roy was transformed into a real devil. The style of acting, however, was rather toned down and normalized in accordance with the adaptation of the text. The more spectacular passages, such as the burning book and the angel's apparition, were solved in magical and impressing ways. They were, in fact "very Steven Spielberg."

As for developing the characters and the choice of actors, the method of acting on the whole was adapted to or was in harmony with the subtle realism in which this company excels. To a certain extent casting reflected an accent on the comic qualities of the play, resulting in several passages of obvious amusement and entertainment, elegantly releasing the play's bright and light tones. The relationship between the characters often took place on a witty, verbal level with less emphasis on direct physical interaction derived from deeper basic tensions (and consequently from a different kind of theatre). Joe was an exception to the brilliant gallery, a tense and restrained person marked by a deficit while Harper had an excess of strength. In general Prior's story became the central one, his sarcasm anchored the production.[12] The "big" drama took priority in the sometimes pompous musical and scenic dimensions.

Millennium Approaches was reviewed in *Politiken* on February 19th. "Maybe longing for seeing a perfect staging of this brilliant play is condemned to fail," Bettina Heltberg states. The central theme in this production is "the fundamental betrayal of love, and the homosexual love between Louis and Prior." Comparing it to the previous production she states that "One misses the crisscrossing of all the persons who touch each other in a permanent search for— well, for what? In the Aarhus version this search obviously was a volcanic, desperate American dream of liberation from oppression, self-oppression as well as social oppression. In the Kongelige Teater production this vital theme is understated." The accent is moved from general themes to individual ones. The "valid and interesting main character" here becomes Louis, due to priority given to the betrayal-of-love theme, and though the Louis/Prior love story is emphasized, it doesn't "swing sensually" between the two of them, and "generally, it is not a particularly sensual performance." Joe's "jump into forbidden homosexual love with Louis" doesn't become a crucial event. Neither does Roy get much significance: "Tony Kushner himself has given much weight to the hateful father figure in the play, Roy Cohn," but only for a few moments did he succeed in taking that position. "(Gay) love's difficult conditions in Reagan's cold America of the '80s" are emphasized by the scenery, which is described as "monumental," a term that is also applied to the staging; it has a negative effect on "the play's fluctuating modern dialectical diagnosis of a sick USA at the end of the millennium," although the humorous breaks and the feverish hallucination of the dance with Louis in act 3, scene 7 make the performance rise.

On the same day, *Berlingske Tidende's* Me Lund developed further her enthusiasm for the play:

"You listen paralysed ... it is not possible to summarize more poetically or toughly the all-devouring insecurity, the vulnerability, the fear of the cynical and inhumane ghost which in the '80s grabbed hold of not only America's Reagan-children but also many of us, who at that time were preparing ourselves to become adults in the transitional phase between two millennia .... Even if it is a gay drama ... it is at the same time *my* world, *my* vulnerability it describes."

Described in a world whose old order has collapsed, and by means of a contemporary scenic language which is atomized, etching. "And it is as such that it finally presents itself in Jan Maagaard's careful staging which ... is cognizant of the entire revolt behind the play, including the way the story is told." The core of the performance is Louis: "with his intelligent acting, his arrogance and uncovered vulnerability he is the focal point in the flickering portrait of our time." The scenery is a "fascinating phallic abstraction, accurately drawing the sterile male universe Kushner's characters live in." "The weaknesses in the production lay in the complicated religious overtones—how seriously should one take them?" and in the characterization of the Mormon couple and of Roy Cohn. With an implicit hint to the Aarhus production Lund states: "Here are no protecting rubber gloves, no myth-making about (closet) gay life, but lots of attacks on conventionalists and spoilsports, liars and love killers and a consequent solidarity with 'victims' ...."[13]

Information's Erik Thygesen wrote on February 20th that two visions in one week raised the heretical question of whether the play is as ingenious as is presumed. His review draws a comparison with the Aarhus version "even if it is not much fun" to have to do so. Where Aarhus had chosen a staging "with smooth passages from the scenes that are realistically narrated to those that are dream or hallucination," accentuation of contrasts, the great, violent, sentimental dimensions and the theatrical, the Kongelige Teater went for the realistic, heavy story of AIDS's influence on a few people in New York, making the characters more average than perhaps suggested by the text. "No one can doubt for a second that Bergenstraahle's version expands to deal with the whole of the USA and the post-war period—Maagaard's is just another story of a closed environment, including one single closet gay and two families, one homosexual and one heterosexual, which dissolve." Thygesen exemplifies the difference between the productions by describing the "kiss of violence" (Roy's kissing of Joe at the end of the play) as being "so brutal that it wouldn't be wrong to call it rape. All the guilt and shame and fear of contagion and homophobia and sexual fear whirls around in the air, concentrated in this one, decisive kiss …. In Copenhagen Cohn clings to Pitt, pulls him towards himself—then Pitt pushes him away, a great and crucial scene reduced to normal drama." The scenic solution is described as "anonymizing costumes (strange considering that an expensive surface appearance was an important part of the Reagan Republicans' victorious style) and the pathetically non-inventive (or should we again say anonymous) New York skyline." In summary, he says that "Bergenstraahle plays in a smaller room but in fact makes the most daring move. Maagaard has got the Kongelige Teater's stage, but makes a cautious move."

In *Weekendavisen* (February 24th), Jens Kistrup talks rather briefly about Maagaard's "normalizing staging which at the same time reveals the play as it is: a rather banal and old-fashioned folkdrama with vivid dialogue but without the depths or secrets a drama must possess in order to really kindle and engage."

A week after *Millennium Approaches*, *Perestroika* had its premiere at the Kongelige Teater.[14] Again small bits of the text had been cut, taking away the most uniquely American references, small "retarding" (self) reflections, including one in act 1, scene 7, where Joe, in the context of a love scene with Louis, declares that "We are a movement, this is politics, not a representation of some pure force, it's … do you want to be pure, or do you want to be effective, choose. Even if our methods seem … extreme, even, we have worked hard to build a movement," which could suggest that Joe is reproducing Roy's way of thinking which he more or less refused in Part One. In the introduction, Tony Kushner says that "*Millennium Approaches* and *Perestroika* are very different plays, and if one is producing them in repertoire the difference should be reflected in their designs." The expression did differ to some extent between the two parts. Of course there were similarities. It might even seem that the comedic tone from Part One turned out to be more appropriate in Part Two, whereas perhaps the melodramatic effects did not. Of course the primary new stage picture was the diorama with its painted landscape quite different from the earlier plastic basic, visual expressions. (The final Bethesda angel was the only other painted set, the background to the Epilogue which presumably is kind of "real." This suggested parallel between the diorama and the painted angel may seem a little bit obscure; or perhaps suggesting a "flat" reality?) The spectacular use of stroboscope light in, for example, Harper's and Joe's meeting in act 4, scene 5 was also different, giving a highly dramatic effect to the scene. Generally the theatrical qualities were emphasized impressively: the ladder to Heaven, Heaven itself, etc. Joe's story was told via the costume change to jeans and more relaxed dressing. As for physical themes—some of them indicated in the text—the staging went a bit further than in Part One. One of the most violent, expressive scenes was the one between Roy and Joe at the hospital (act 4, scene 1) when Roy rises from the bed, tears off the drop, begins to bleed significantly, and ends up clinging to Joe, leaving a lot of infected blood on his shirt. During Belize's description of heaven (act 3, scene 4) Roy masturbates in the bed (maybe without the obvious relation to the theme). When Harper asks Joe what he sees after having sex, she stands up naked in the bed (act 4, scene 7).

Part Two was, of course, received by the critics in comparison to both Part One and the Aarhus version. *Politiken* was the only paper that did not have the same critic review all of the different performances. Instead of Bettina Heltberg, Monna Dithmer (younger generation) did the review on March 5th. There is more life here than in the somewhat static Part One, she states. She describes the essence of Prior's prophetic message as "Follow your heart's longings." But the performance, to some extent, lets its own message down. It surely masters the witty-cynical style, according to "Tony Kushner's dramatic construction which has every emotional culmination accompanied by a humorous break, a down-to-earth distance. But that doesn't mean that Kushner's angels are without feelings." The erotic relationships are seen as rather "non-sensual, even though the bodies are exposed in the nude."[15] "Even if *Angels in America* is a vital revolt against homophobia and American national idealism, in this production the play is weakened by its own angel-phobia ... and thereby it cancels out the whole spiritual dimension from the play's emotional register .... As a revelation, the production is short on magic and vision, a poor message for the AIDS-struck prophet to bring to a time afraid of emotions."

To the contrary, on the same date in *Berlingske Tidende*, Me Lund states that Part Two was heavier than Part One. Its message is man's responsibility for his own life: "Are we able to change?" She compares Part Two with the London production where it seemed a relief after the darker first part, even if she has difficulties with the religious dimension. "It was overwhelming and life-affirming in the midst of tragedy." Lund blames slow tempo for not obtaining the same experience, not exploiting the wit and irony.

Erik Thygesen in *Information* (March 3rd), states that in Part Two the foreign historical-political background becomes a real problem. "For a Danish audience it is an intellectual, not an emotional exercise to experience a parallel between the '50s McCarthyism and fear of communism and the '80s Reaganism and fear of AIDS. For an American audience it is presumably a shock to see Ethel Rosenberg meet Roy Cohn in an AIDS story. For a Danish audience which hardly remembers the Rosenberg family and has not heard about Roy Cohn before Kushner placed him in his play, it is difficult to be swept along with the emotion, so you very easily begin to focus on the play's weaknesses." The religious level is "superficial stage business." What really impresses are scenes that communicate on other levels: Joe and Louis in bed with each other ("We have seen lots of exaggerated and screaming gays, but mature men who just enjoy being together—very rarely"); the diorama scenes with their contrast between the rigid tableaus and the characters' confrontations; the grotesque confrontation between the dying, prejudiced Cohn and Belize, "a nurse who is black, male and gay, far away from the closet." The principal impression is that the production has moved the play only slightly from its original background.

Jens Kistrup in *Weekendavisen* (March 17th) focuses on political aspects, how to create a contemporary political theatre. He does not see an obvious relationship between the gay and the political themes in Part Two, with its messages that you must accept yourself and that a change is possible. But the production presents itself as just another (post-political) version of the story of American lies of life à la O'Neill, Miller, etc., the angels "just being a stage trick which the theatre hardly tries to take seriously."

Just like in Aarhus, the production of both parts in Copenhagen reached its audience. The audience figures were very high.

In conclusion it may be said—by way of simplification—that by being unfaithful to the text, even if every single word is respected, the Aarhus version transferred some of its controversy, even though in other registers, simply because the original ones would not have made sense in a Danish context, as mentioned above. Conversely, the Copenhagen version payed more respect to the American universe and so came closer to a normal theatre event, though it was a great and spectacular one, and thus reached a broad audience. Both theatres failed, for different reasons, to approach the angelic dimension's hell, whatever that may be.

Finally, the logo angel from Aarhus was nude, crouching, pointing downwards, its face covered by black hair, slightly enigmatic; the Copenhagen angel was hovering, bright, light, raising upwards, beautiful and beautifully dressed. Flying in different directions. However, even this simplification dissolves when we consider the reviewers' reception; the number of directions proves to be legion.

Notes

1. In the Scandinavian countries there are very large differences in, for instance, religion and morality. Thus, in the Norwegian version of the play presented by National teatret, Oslo in 1994, directed by Edith Roger, the homosexual dimension was treated with "protective rubber gloves," according to Me Lund in *Berlingske Tidende*, April 12, 1994. In fact, the theatre had asked a professor in Theology to write an article about the play, in which he described it as "a kind of religious mystery play in which people in the midst of their fragile and treacherous lives to their own astonishment fight the struggle of faith ...," as well as posing questions such as, "do piety and homosexuality exclude each other?" In Sweden the first staged production of the play (after a radio production) was produced at Stockholm's Stadsteater, in 1995, directed by the alternative and experimental theatre director, Richard Günther.

2. Of course a basic fascination with the occult prevails. David Lynch's *Twin Peaks* was a cult phenomenon. The music in the Aarhus production of *Angels in America* contained some references to *Twin Peaks* (see below).

3. It has to be said that since the 1980s' banishment of politics from the stage in this part of the world, treating political issues in a theatrical form in itself is controversial. In that perspective *Angels in America* is a taboo-breaker, and a potential opening for

a re-discovery of certain themes. That is, especially the kinds of re-discovery which involve narrative techniques and expressions referring to "wild" theatre experiments that theoretically are in opposition to conventional "political" theatre.

4. The traces of meaning in the names are found again in Harper *Amaty* Pitt. The super-example, of course, is that the great Father and King is called Roy—only he happens to refer to a non-fictitious universe (which thus also interferes).

5. Designer: Anette Hansen; Composer: Soeren Dahl; Translator: Jacob Kielland; based on the version produced by the Royal National Theatre, London; published by Nick Hern Books.

6. In the light of such scenes, the suggestion that the production toned down its gay theme (see the reception referred to below) seems rather meaningless. The reviews indicate that the main difference between the two productions, is whether it is primarily Joe's or Louis's story that is told. However this cannot be discussed without reference to the scenic presence of the actual actors; as is always the case in theatre. Even Joe's story is a (closet) gay story! Giving Harper femininity is not a negation of this; on the contrary it corroborates it.

7. See Kushner's *Note About the Staging* which recommends "scene shifts done rapidly," and adds that "the moments of magic—the appearance and disappearance of Mr. Lies and the ghosts, the Book hallucination, and the ending—are to be fully realized as bits of wonderful *Theatrical* illusion, which means it's OK if the wires show, and maybe it's good they do, but the magic should at the same time be thoroughly amazing." No doubt these are words of general value, but in the individual, different cases it might seem appropriate to ask more specific questions, such as "What is the Angel to the character(s) and to the audience?," "What kind of visual universe does it, eventually, refer to?" An angel is not just an angel. It has to be cast, costumed, etc.

8. These choices happen in order to respect the author's indications. The criticism is not repeated in connection with the Kongelige Teater's production (see below) even if it used exactly the same practice. It is remarkable that where the former critic finds the political theme the central one, Lund focuses on the loss of or lack of meaning. This may reflect a generational difference, but it is funny that the younger one insists on conventional

logic when she emphasizes the theme of "modern civilization's break down."

9. Since the critic underlines the American angle it may seem a paradox that he, alone, criticizes the preservation of references to American names. It might be argued that with another paradox, the more specific the performance's universe was, the more general it became (as demonstrated by the fact that the dialogue never was "normalized") and thus again generated a poetic universe of its own. The next production, by the Kongelige Teater, used exactly this method: it removed the mentioned references and made the dialogue more "natural," as described below.

10. This reminds the critic of the speaker without a speech at the end of Ionesco's *The Chairs*.

11. Set Designer: Mats Persson; Costumes: Tine Sander; Translator: Morti Vizki; based on the same text as the Aarhus production.

12. This, of course, is my interpretation. As seen below some critics considered Louis to be the central character. Thank God (Mormon? Aleph?) there is no absolutely true answer, but rather, a number of experiences! Consequently I have chosen to modify my own observations by involving some reviews.

13. The glove metaphor figured in a number of reviews. I quote one of those not discussed here, namely *BT*, February 19th, by Birgitte Grue, "The play's central gay point-of-view in Johan Bergenstraahle's Aarhus staging is toned down, but if, in Aarhus, they handle the gay theme with velvet gloves, in Copenhagen they do it with asbestos gloves, for Jan Maagaard's very smooth and melodramatic staging rather suffers from fear of touching!" It is remarkable that the classical formula for "political" theatre—negative vs. positive—seems to appeal more to Lund than the Aarhus version, which, according to, for instance, Erik Thygesen (see above) was more complicated; for him it was a personal challenge to be confronted with a Roy Cohn you had to feel for.

14. This involved the same staff as the production of Part One. The translation was based on Final Draft, November 18, 1993.

15. This refers to Joe and Louis.

Historical Revue
and Dance of Death

by Franz Wille

Nicki van Tempelhoff and Zazie de Paris
in *Engel in America*. Photo © Matthias Horn.

Part of the success is a tendency of the characters to enjoy talking, to express themselves, or what they believe themselves to be, completely and totally, which with their high level of stress takes some considerable time. In any event, in German this takes longer than in English and in productions true to the text, such as those in Zurich, Hamburg and Essen, this leads to playing times, even at a forced tempo, of between three and a half and four hours.

For the comparative critic this means that already by the second production a creeping satiety sets in—"I know what you mean"—for which you can only partially blame Tony Kushner, since audiences who subject themselves to four or more consecutive *Angels* are certainly not his target audience.

For the actor it means: No lengthy subcutaneous searches in complicated inner worlds, but instead to portray characters with clear gestures which neither stand in the way of the detailed dialogue nor unnecessarily repeat it. The productions in Zurich, Hamburg, Essen and Frankfurt are all linked, despite their many differences, by a series of "aha" effects. An entrance, a posture, a sentence, a turn and so it is decided: In this way and in no other is Joe or Harper, Louis or Prior imagined here.

The Mafia advocate in the White House

Take Roy Cohn, the only historical character in the play. The son of a reasonably serious New York judge, he learned early what is important if all that matters is success. "I don't want to know what the law is. I want to know who's the judge," is his alleged legal principle (although it is not stated in the play). He has allegedly never had a real collection of law books in his chambers. Instead he worked from early in his career as the main advisor to McCarthy's Senate committee on un-American activities with a web of connections, dependencies, bribery and irresistible bossiness towards "friends of society" in the courts, the executive branch and the Mafia. This network allowed him for 30 years to achieve amazing court decisions beyond all legal reasoning as well as to withstand all attacks by the Department of Justice and several justified charges. He neither camouflaged nor concealed nor repressed his own homosexuality. It simply didn't exist in his world and that was enough for him—and his world. Which is why he was able to hold court with his pleasure boys on a yacht and simultaneously fight most effectively against equal rights for homosexuals. Among his clients were Norman Mailer, Frank Sinatra, Edgar Hoover, Donald Trump, Richard Nixon, Ronald Reagan and several Mafia godfathers.

In Zurich, Christian Schneller plays Roy Cohn as you might imagine a nasty, ambitious American lawyer, if you mainly know about nasty, ambitious American lawyers from lousy American TV series: Energetic on the phone, tight movements, firm intonation and all the while he is elegant and always superior. Schneller's Cohn stays cleverly within these common conventions, which one assumes could be true even if one knows they probably aren't. In this way we can all let ourselves be deceived—not the worst option. The direction by Volker Hesse is appropriate to the poverty of a small, badly funded and culturally embattled theatre as he relies on the *virtue* of superficial but sharp acting. Thus, he makes nothing conspicuously false and therefore much is correct. The rest is the play.

In Werner Schroeter's direction at Hamburg's Deutsches Schauspielhaus, Matthias Fuchs plays Roy Cohn, and the question that arises here is whether no one there watches lousy American TV series. The Hamburg Cohn wears what is presumably meant to be an especially hip, screamingly colourful suit, and stands by his desk, which is outfitted with a flashing digital console in its legs (set and costume design by Alberte Barsacq). On the phone, he obligingly chats people up like a greasy bell hop. Whoever Roy Cohn may have been, he certainly would not have been successful if no one could have taken him seriously, let alone fear him.

Angels in Hamburg—A Steeplechase

In several respects Schroeter's production in Hamburg offers the alternative program to the one in Neumarkt. While in the cramped space of the Züricher Theater, the scenes are performed drily, in front of or next to the audience, using a raised stage (Marietta Eggmann) which diagonally divides the room, the wide stage of the Deutsches Schauspielhaus is dominated by a monumental, half-abstract stage picture created by interlocking platforms in front of a stylized New York skyscraper right out of Legoland. In the middle there is a pool sufficiently large to allow for wading—for reasons only known to the program notes. There is a photo with the informative subtitle "Lunch break in New York": A couple of business people chew on their hamburgers (the American variety) sitting on the rim of a fountain, a stimulus which seems to have landed the set designer in shallow water.

In front of this monumental set where human scale is degraded, on a stage the crossing of which resembles a steeplechase, the actors often seek safety near the apron and mainly in large, if false, emotions. Barbara Nüsse as the pill-popping Harper frustrated with her marriage, appears on stage with straggly hair, deep furrows in her face, and plays an equally moving and repulsive nervous wreck whose mere presence would drive any life-partner to the very same hell. You therefore understand her fugitive husband all too well, while, on the other hand, you're surprised that a woman, obviously over fifty, here cast as a young wife, can so self-evidently fear a pregnancy.

Contrary to any clue in the text, her husband Joe is, in Stephan Bissmeir's performance, some fifteen years younger (that is, unless you believe the old wives' tale according to which a closet homosexual man tends to fall in love with older women who are presumably not erotically dangerous, which in Barbara Nüsse's case, in any event, doesn't become clear either). He confines himself to slow speech, to a wooden awkwardness and a pinstriped stiffness, which leaves Roy's passion for him all the more bewildering. Indeed, the main problem in Schroeter's production is the homo-eroticism, this passion that is still discriminated against, which Tony Kushner's play wants to/should bring into public domain without any aggressive confessionalism. As *magnus*'s critic, Axel Schock complains, "It is as if the actors were defending themselves from their characters; they let go of their roles without ever performing them. You don't sense their gayness at all (on the contrary) and so when Louis picks up a man in the park and begs to get fucked, the scene has barely a hint of eroticism, only much helpless mechanics."

Zazie de Paris, as the loathsome, overly Frenchified nurse with slipping reading glasses ogling Prior's fever chart as if she wanted to whip the naughty boy's behind, confidently sidesteps such close-to-life criticism and thereby transplants *Angels in America* to where it least of all belongs: in the middle-class fantasy land of a transsexual

honky-tonk. The final entrance of the angel, Kushner's daring mixing of redemption-myth and Hollywood apotheosis, is transformed
by Zazie and her director, using strains of Verdi, into a final intensi-
fication of mendacious, dripping kitsch. As a pathetically inspired
housewife with femme-fatale ambitions, she cranes on the back of a
patient who falters under the weight and so delivers the production's
unmasking, final symbolic tableau: crushed under unbearably good
intentions.

Homo-eroticism à la Essen

Roy Cohn number three. In Essen, Claus Boysen plays the New York
power broker with the tubby energy of a middle-class entrepreneur
who blathers to his opposite number in friendly joviality as if he had
to bring his customers a huge assortment of water faucets. Even the
most incredible lines from the AIDS-infected lawyer, who uses the
most evil threats to browbeat his doctor into diagnosing him with
liver cancer, feel like forbearing advice from a hearty boss. Under
Jürgen Bosse's direction this company doesn't rely on the American
television world either but rather on the provinciality of their own
minds as they put their trust in a literal reading of the text which at
times leads to curious events.

The lawyer, Joe, whose exact occupation is given as "chief clerk
for a justice of the federal court of appeal," seems to have a title
which sounds like a bureaucratic invention, but as the chief of staff
who, among other things, writes decisions for the justice, he actually
pulls the strings in the background. Peter Rühring lends him the flair
of a middle-aged bookkeeper who only lacks sleeve protectors to be
completely happy, and whose erotic desires are only aroused by
rows of three-ring binders. His depressive wife, Harper, on the other
hand appears as an unlucky child with shadowy eyes, who is immediately believed when she says that her marriage is only breaking
down because of him, which—from the perspective of a divorce
court justice—settles the question of blame fairly easily and, in
contrast to the Hamburg production, completely reverses the blame.
And so again the men bear all the blame, which we
already suspected ...

The secret lead-character of the play is the AIDS-infected Prior Walter, who with sure instinct for the right moment chooses his partner Louis's grandmother's funeral to reveal that he suffers from the incurable disease. While in Zürich and Hamburg two young men, who are as internationally good looking as designer jeans, live against death with an enraged helpless despair, which their theatricality can never fully deny, Thomas Goritzki in Essen abandons every attempt to stylize the doomed man into a seductive icon of sacrifice. He gives his character an unobtrusive symptomatology, does not search for the usual New York liveliness, but surrounds Prior with a bit of old-fashioned, self-congratulatory conviviality, a petty bourgeois in striped pyjamas, who lolls about at home in front of the baroque mirror in lush rags, but who could be imagined, with his shower-safe perm, after soccer on Saturdays, tilting back a Pilsener at the corner pub: An angel in the Ruhr Valley. However, even the best-grounded emotional weights have their price. Prior's dry self-ironical statements become increasingly blunted.

The most dangerous therapy for Kushner's *Angels* lies in concentrated doses of empathetic acting. The unbelievable horror expressed in autobiographical accounts of illness written by people like Hervé Guibert and Wolfgang Max Faust, seems not to have been grasped by Kushner's play. The impact of *Angels in America* is too recognizable, too craftsmanly calculated to properly convey real death. The more internally the actors approach their characters the more glaringly sweaty the melodramatic places threaten to become, the more obtrusively these private dramas turn into emotional blackmail which discredits the political motives of the writer from behind.

A Radical Cure at Schauspiel Frankfurt

At the Schauspiel Frankfurt, Thomas Schulte-Michels has dared a radical cure against such dangers. The text has been heavily cut, the performance lasts, without intermission, one and three-quarter hours, the rest is told by the actors. Any effort at emotional illusion is killed in the light of the follow-spots and by the use of microphones or microports which all participants make thorough use of. Any attempt at empathy is coldly sent packing by lightning speech tempi, gangling-cool show-entrances and occasional confranciersingsong. Needless remnants of sympathy are taken care of by the ensemble, as among all the possible qualities of their characters they choose those that blend least well together, often the least pleasant.

On Susanne Thaler's apron-wide forestage of a brocade-red landscape of cushions in front of a gleaming green drop, Roy Cohn, alias Hans Falár, struts about as a dangerous effeminate telephone-virtuoso in patent-leather shoes, letting his favourite Joe starve by his arm as he offers him delicate tidbits. This doesn't overly impress Christoph Hohmann, one hand in his pocket, the other holding a microphone, as he converses with the audience in equal measure on the narrow strip under the iron curtain hanging barely three meters above. The overt intentions of the play are not forced into pseudo-realistic character psychology, rather they are often—and without the camouflage so much more convincingly—illustrated.

Wolfgang Koch's Louis is clearly differentiated from his Zürich, Hamburg, or Essen models, who more or less strained to imitate Woody Allen's nervous-sympathetic, city neurotic image. This eloquent, witty, Jewish intellectual does not palaver away in a continuous hectic, comical tone about his fear of his lover's illness and his feelings of guilt over leaving him. As he begs his doomed friend who has just collapsed in his own excrement, "don't become more sick," this does not sound like a senseless, sentimental phrase, but just as absurd as this demand after all is—and therefore unexpectedly despairing. Louis and Prior already know the score when the word "kaposi" is uttered, a glance between them suffices; all false hopes of being saved, any denial of fact are made superfluous. And when Prior then says that he is afraid that Louis now will leave him, the "small pause" indicated in the stage directions means that for the first time his fears have hit the bull's eye.

Günter Lampe plays Prior without artifice as the older man who fears for his considerably younger lover and from the beginning knows that he has no chance of keeping him. In the scene where Prior, already displaying symptoms of his illness, puts on the transvestite rags alone one more time, he puts on so much make-up that he looks like a corpse—without the melancholy or vanity which would have turned a touching moment into a tear-jerker. And Joe knows from the beginning that he is gay. When he speaks with Harper about their breaking marriage, his excuses are one large admission of things that cannot be denied and in his confessional call in the night to his mother he doesn't attempt to be coquette with the worst of all possibilities, for a puritanically brought up Mormon. There's no pseudo-provocation to test her reaction, rather he establishes a fact with frank objectivity, before which even the most mendacious façade of morality must capitulate.

In Frankfurt, they are saying with the most sober naturalness that homosexuality is certainly not something natural, that one need not say *more* about it than there is to say, and that Kushner's "Gay Fantasia on National Themes," as its subtitle describes it, in our tolerant society perhaps doesn't elucidate anything new, but this kind of tolerance is certainly not a sign of enlightenment. So long as that is necessary for the theme, it will remain a theme.

Angels in Australia

by Ian Olorenshaw

Joe Pitt (Joe Stone) and Roy Cohn (Jacek Koman) in the Melbourne
Theatre Company production of *Angels in America, Part One: Millenium
Approaches*. Photo © Jeff Busby.

Angels in Australia

by Ian Olorenshaw

The phenomenon of *Angels in America* in Australia reminds me very much of a visiting muscled Adonis at the gym. He is big, gay, fantastically formed, hyper-masculine, strong and physically adorable. This particular American, let's call him Todd, is also charming, witty, intelligent, glamorous, worldly, educated, articulate, highly camp and very 'gay scene'. His education enables him to talk to many who also have knowledge of, and an interest in, his particular kind of America. His strength and physical attraction imbue him with the power to be accessible to those he chooses to be, whilst being intimidating and inaccessible to some because of the very attributes that make him so attractive. Whilst in Australia he wins many awards. The Australians who sponsor him also achieve recognition for their part in his success. Of course being HIV-positive and an angryactivistloudaboutit subjects him to various responses. Some Australians admire, love and desire him, others, afraid of his HIV and intellectual status, neglect or refuse to meet him, afraid of being hurt. His specific nationality, sexuality and identification with the gay community is significant.

Todd symbolizes aspects of an Australian response to an American play. *Angels in America* represents an American world full of the problems arising out of the confrontation with HIV and AIDS. How closely do Australians identify with the problems faced by

IAN OLORENSHAW is a theatre practitioner and post-graduate student in the Department of Theatre Studies, University of New England, Armidale, where he is undertaking research into Queer theory and practice.

Americans in America? What impact has *Angels in America* had on Australia? I want to make the distinction between *Angels in America*'s constructive attempt as theatre to participate in the development of queer discourse, and its embeddedness in its own American milieu. This distinction gives the plays both a usefulness to an international discourse, and a fictional life of hyper-real theatricality. There is no doubt in my mind that the Melbourne Theatre Company (MTC) production was a spectacular event. It is true that the vast majority of critics in the media enthusiastically acknowledge that *Angels* was authoritative, alluring and influential theatre.This, balanced with little or no public controversy and/or debate in Melbourne and Adelaide, suggests a fairly widespread acknowledgment of the productions' excellence and, one would assume, appeal. The following discussion seeks to discover why such eagerly anticipated theatre, regarded as a phenomenon, is produced here, is undoubtedly a critical and artistic success, yet does not sell out any of its seasons. A possibility surely within its reach.

Angels in America's existence here has had an interesting maturation. Scheduled to coincide with the Sydney Gay and Lesbian Mardi Gras, both parts were produced in February 1993 by the Sydney Theatre Company (STC), in the Wharf Theatre—the smaller of its two main theatres—under the direction of Michael Gow, a noted Australian playwright. It must also be noted that Sydney saw both parts produced together before New York and London.

In October and November 1993, Neil Armfield directed the MTC production of *Millennium Approaches* with some critical complaints that it suffered in the 'cramped', now closed Russell Street Theatre. In September 1994, Armfield directed both parts—including Kushner's re-writing of Part Two—in repertory in the more spacious Playhouse in The Victorian Arts Centre. In October 1994, MTC toured Part One to the Adelaide Festival Centre, under the mantle of the State Theatre of South Australia. What was advertised to be a moved reading of *Perestroika* became more or less one full performance. Neil Armfield introduced the performance. Bill Phillips, in his review for the *Adelaide Gay Times*, described this "prologue [as] quite Shakespearean in content."

> He begged our indulgence for any deficiencies, praised the efforts of cast and crew, and explained the circumstances of this unusual event. He was charming, and set a tone

that had the audience with the actors every step of the way from the first scene.

Very Quince!

Bums on Seats

Angels' six week season in Sydney was produced as an exclusive event outside of the company's main subscription season, consequently without the advantage of a pre-paid audience base. It achieved 55.8% total attendance of capacity. To make a brief comparison with the plays in the subscription season, only one achieved less than 75% of attendance, whilst six were over 80% and another reached 97%.[1] It is significant, I think, to mention here again that the STC season of *Angels* coincided with the Sydney Gay and Lesbian Mardi Gras, arguably Australia's largest public event, attracting huge international attention, and involving many arts exhibitions and activities. With this in mind it would be quite reasonable to ask why, when the Sydney media reviews generally lauded the production, it did not attract larger audiences despite the lack of a subscription base. Headlines like "Dazzling, Visionary Drama" (Rosemary Neill) and "Astounding *Angels*" (Stephen Dunne) and the accompanying enthusiastic reviews seemed to overshadow Leo Schofield's comments that "[Michael Gow] has saddled himself and the piece with what may well be the ugliest, most inhibiting set I've seen in years" (February 27). Many who were able to contrast both the Sydney and Melbourne productions agreed. Schofield made his comparison with London's National Theatre's production of Part One (February 13).

The MTC production of Part One in 1993 achieved a total paid capacity of 80%. Of this 50% were subscriptions and 30% were general public. Comparatively the three other subscription productions in the Russell Street Theatre achieved, 58%, 75% and 74% paid capacity.[2] On a percentage basis *Angels in America* attracted less subscriptions than the others but more than 50% more general public. Brenton Kewley, MTC's audience development manager, is quoted as saying that "the subscription audience for *Millennium Approaches* was low and that most of the general public ticket sales came from university ranks and the homosexual community" (Olb 35). In 1994 the figures are significantly different. One must take into account the change of venue, the capacity of which was more than double. Paid capacity here for both parts was 45%, of which 28% was subscription and 17% general public. The general public sales for the three other productions in the Playhouse in this subscription season were the same or up to five points higher.[3]

The State Theatre of South Australia produced Part One of *Angels in America* which achieved 56.2% of paid capacity. The single charity performance of *Perestroika*, for the AIDS Council of South Australia, achieved 60% of capacity of which nine tenths—a very rough estimate—were gay men. It is important to note that *Angels* was the least subscribed of the season in South Australia and that the State Theatre received a number of letters of complaint from their subscribers. Warwick Tiernan, the company publicist notes that "While there were complaints about language and sexual content generally, others were more specific in their criticism of the choice of play and the representation of homosexuality on stage."[4] In the public media, however, it was critically acclaimed.

Whilst marketing of the productions was directed at the mainstream, strong emphasis was given to targeting the gay community. It is impossible to tell what percentage of the audiences were identifying members of the gay and lesbian communities, but as Warwick Tiernan puts it, "there are a number as we know from observation (!) and anecdotal evidence."

Reviews and Responses

Pre-production publicity emphasizes the contemporaneous nature of *Angels in America*. It stresses the "universality" of the play whilst implicitly and explicitly acknowledging its Americanness. Just what does *Angels in America* have to offer Australians apart from riveting theatre? Critics in the media and theatre practitioners are almost unanimous about both the Sydney and Melbourne productions' quality. This was expressed in the print media and through its awards. The 1993 MTC production of *Millennium Approaches* received a swag of Melbourne's most prestigious theatre awards, including being voted by critics as the theatrical highlight of 1993. It received the Green Room awards, presented in Melbourne, for Best Production, Best Director (Neil Armfield), Best Actor (David

Tredinnick), Best Supporting Actor (Jacek Koman) and Best Light-
ing Design (Rory Dempster). And in 1994 *Perestroika* was also
bathed in acclamation and awards. It received the Green Room
Awards for Best Production, Best Director (Neil Armfield), and Best
Actor (Melvin J Carroll). Jacek Komen received The Age Performing
Arts Award for Best Performance in 1994 for both Parts One and
Two.[5] But critics of both the Sydney and Melbourne productions of
Part Two were less enthusiastic saying it did not reach the heights of
Part One. Jason Romney of the Herald Sun gave *Millennium Ap-
proaches* five stars, and its sequel three.

The unfortunate thing for *Angels*, the thing that is the substance
and subject of its greatness, its Americanness, is also its undoing.
Almost no Australian would be unfamiliar with things American.
American production is deeply ingrained within Australian society.
On television particularly we are subjected to American movies,
sitcoms, news and advertising. Our cinemas overflow with American
films. The problems *Angels in America* deals with are specifically
American; its culturality is American; its ethnicity is American, then
necessarily its gaze is American. The plays make no secret of their
Americanness and most critics show an explicit recognition of it.
Many critics felt the need to enlighten their readers as to the identity
of Roy Cohn. In her review of MTC's 1993 production, Felicity
Bloch of the Australian Jewish News emphasizes how specifically
American the situations are that she describes. She discusses
"*America*'s irreducible ethnic diversity ..." and the representation of
Mormons who are "... a timely reminder that visionary religious
cults are embedded in *America*'s historical traditions" (my empha-
ses). She explained to her mostly Jewish readers the person of Roy
Cohn and his part in "the convictions of the Rosenbergs ...." Her
narrative assumes the readers' knowledge of the Rosenbergs, but not
of Roy Cohn. It might be fair then to assume that if Jewish readers
are aware of the Rosenbergs, and not of Roy Cohn, then non-Jewish
Australians are less likely to know who he is, or the Rosenbergs for
that matter, unless one has a specific knowledge of the history. She
re-emphasizes Roy Cohn's biography in her 1994 review of both
parts. Helen Thomson notes in the *Australian* that:

> All of his [Kushner's] characters are afflicted, lost, con-
> fused victims of ideologies and beliefs, but all identify
> themselves as united in their Americanness, a concept

> which turns out to be as elusive as that of the "normal" …
> these people are patients awaiting liberation and cure
> from the condition of being late-20th Century Americans.

As Roy Cohn is heard to repeat, "Only in America" (*Millennium Approaches* 15).

Bill Phillips writing in Adelaide, wrote ecstatic reviews of both parts for the *Adelaide Gay Times*, and presented a rhapsodic paper to the Uranian Society, a cultural group of gay men into the arts. His feelings about the plays' Americanness are expressed in this extract from the address:

> We are so steeped in an American milieu we can hardly
> help identify anyway, particularly having taken our
> liberative lead from the fag movement of the '70s and '80s.

The lead up to the 1994 production was grabbed by the gay press with the expected enthusiasm. Crusader Hillis introduces the liftout:

> *Melbourne Star Observer* is proud to bring you this special
> eight-page liftout featuring both *Angels in America*, and
> the people who are bringing it to life in Melbourne … plus
> an exclusive calendar so that you can plan your participa-
> tion in the theatre event of the year. (19 August 1994)

In *Brother Sister,* one of Melbourne's gay papers, Geoffrey Williams gives a singularly enthusiastic review stressing that *Millennium Approaches* is "one of the most important plays of the decade." The following year in the same publication Laurie Lane gives this enthu-siastic final paragraph:

> If the audience reaction tonight is anything to go by then
> Tony Kushner and this highly skilled team of actors got
> the message across loud and clear with a resounding
> smash.

The message of which Lane speaks seems to be hope for the realiza-tion of a queer nation. One must also wonder why such audience enthusiasm was not passed on and seen to affect the box office results. Suzanne Olb, writing for the Victorian Arts Centre Magazine, *Stages*, interviewed some prominent "homosexual" audience members. She quotes Boris Kaspiev as saying:

The thing that hit me most was the politics and the way politics creates the backdrop against which ordinary people live their lives ... American nationalism and the influence of American conservative right-wing politics comes through very clearly and is juxtaposed with some elements of fantasy and the bizarre. ... very much a part of American life ... this was America: conservative, fantastic, and bizarre all rolled into one.

Many critics make claims to *Angels'* universal themes. If *Angels in America* does offer Australians a "universal" message, is it what John Larkin, in *The Sunday Age* has observed in the play to be "the constant need for vigilance to protect society against cynicism, opportunism, and personal weakness in the face of adversity"? In the same article Larkin points out:

Those who may wonder what such work has to do with Australians have only to remember, especially in the 1980s, how susceptible this society has been to manipulation in the name of power, and realize the resonances with "a world of no connections, no responsibilities," as shown in the play.

But do we need *Angels in America* to remind us of this? If we do, several thousand Australians for whom there were empty seats regrettably missed it. In his 1994 review of both plays Larkin makes the assertion that the plays are

... a remarkable and audacious mixing of realism and non-naturalistic styles. The result leaves a long trail of vivid impressions and responses that refuses to let us alone merely to sit in the theatre and imagine we are being entertained, despite the comfort of the humour and the delusion that it really has nothing to do with us.

Do the themes that *Angels in America* articulates reflect Australia's politics, Australia's identity, or in fact Australia's concerns? I am convinced that *Angels in America* as a theatrical event had much to offer Australians; however the audience responses seem to indicate that what *Angels* had to offer audiences as gay political theatre, is not what Australians, or even gay Australians altogether wanted to see.

The personal responses are harder to gauge but I approached several acquaintances whom I knew to be theatre-goers, but not necessarily with an education related to theatre or criticism. Of these gay men, who offered informal coffee-table responses, one saw only the 1993 version of Part One. He said that he felt the production was not well handled, that the Angel's wings looked too fake, and that there seemed to be a hurried intensity to the show, perhaps trying to live up to MTC's passion for voluminous production, trying to achieve too much in the space available. He also felt that the play was directed at what he thought to be the subscription audience, the conservative "blue rinse" set. As it was being produced by a state theatre company, Victoria's most heavily funded and subscribed theatre company, its sense of elitism alienated him.

His boyfriend who enjoyed the production very much did not feel alienated by the AIDS theme but felt the show to be very sombre. He identified with the character of Joe Pitt—being of a similar age—and his difficulty in coming out, but otherwise felt the show did not strike much of a chord with him and was consequently not particularly interested in seeing Part Two. He did make the point that having only recently come out, he had not known and still did not know anyone with, or who had died from HIV/AIDS.

An Adelaide friend saw Part One only. He loved it, finding it stimulating and thought provoking. When questioned about why he thought it did not attract a larger audience, he suggested that it had an exclusive appeal, that it was expensive, and that there was probably not the population to support it. He was aware of the advertised reading of Part Two, but decided he would not go because he felt that Part One had ended well, and that he could not manage the expense for something he had every reason to believe would only be a reading.

There is no doubt that *Angels in America* was received with enthusiasm by the critics and extremely varied personal responses. Could its Americanness have contributed to discouraging attendance? Let us look further.

Fantastic Production

Neil Armfield's acclaimed direction produced extravagant shows for Melbourne. The large backdrop resembled a tempestuous sky. Within the Playhouse's proscenium arch all ropes and pulleys were clearly visible and almost every stage object was on wheels enabling the cast members to smoothly and swiftly run them in and out. There were two large rotatable flats set on each side of the stage, like wings, resembling the dark stony nature of Central Park's public toilets and monuments. The productions' animation created the frenetic society America seems to be. It is a hyper-activity or neurosis that seemed to pervade all the characterizations; apparently a symptom of a society that has lost its way, ethically, morally and socially.

How could one not be affected by the sight of the torrential blood flow as Jacek Komen's Roy Cohn tore the drip from his arm? The beat between the wrenching of the needle and the appearance of the gushing blood was impeccably timed and repellent. Totally engrossing also was watching David Tredinnick's Prior Walter lose bowel control. The recognition of the shit-stained blood, or blood-stained shit seeping through his pyjamas was exacting. Greg Stone's lovable characterization of the Mormon Joe Porter Pitt, the well mannered, cutely accented, boy next door, exemplifies the closeted conservative. With his Mormon marriage and sexual preference in conflict, he is trapped within and advocating the machinations of both juridical and religious forces. Catherine McClements's portrayal of his valium addicted wife was convincingly Mormon-oriented, and clearly conveyed confusion about her husband's sexual preference. In fact all of the characters in *Angels* were so skilfully portrayed that there was no doubt of the effect the American government's repugnant attitude towards HIV/AIDS and sexuality in general, now as in the eighties, has on all of them. Monica Maughan comically portrayed a small, endearing, supernatural and delightfully vengeful Ethel Rosenberg. Her large Hannah Pitt, from Salt Lake City, was assertive and humane, and who could forget the moment when she kisses Margaret Mills' stunning Angel. William McClusky's Rabbi and Bolshevik, Aleksii Antedilluvianovich Prelapsarianov are undeniably, and unequivocally American constructs. Colin Batrouney, both actor and activist, played Louis, giving us a potent reminder of the ideological rhetoric which can consume and confuse the mind leading to complete ineffectuality. And then there is Melvin Carroll's exciting portrayal of Belize and Mr. Lies. Leonard Radic in fact made the point in his review of the 1993 production:

> The scene in which the latter listens patiently while Louis lectures him on race, tolerance and the virtues of American society and then lets him down with a thud, is one of the best scenes in both the play and the production.

How is a production that is so all-American made accessible to an Australian audience? Firstly the MTC programme includes a glossary which provides such important information as personal biographies of people referred to or characterized in the play, including the Rosenbergs, and Presidents Reagan and Bush. It explains initials like AIDS, HIV, AZT, CMV (Cytomegalovirus), and KS (Kaposi's Sarcoma). A whole page of the programme quotes from R. Pearson's obituary of Roy M. Cohn published in *The Washington Post* including a photograph taken in 1986 of the very sick man. This page also includes Kushner's disclaimer. The realization of the necessity for such a glossary suggests an explicit Americanness.

Armfield and his wholly strong cast and crew created an extravagant stage event. The whole stage setting for both productions was large, exaggerated and fulfilling. The raw emotional power created by an apparently effortless but terrifying descent of the Angel was enough to induce tears. The onslaught of graphic imagery was altogether moving. *Angels'* Melbourne productions are consistent with the critics' responses. They survived on the writing, the stagecraft, the immense power of the actors and exquisitely discharged direction. The magic realism in the dream and hallucination scenes expertly staged by the Australian practitioners made for an electrifying show. I think such a production, regardless of its racial, political or national background and agenda, deserved an audience for its contribution to art and spectacle. Yet it does have a political agenda. Its politics have already been observed by the critics, and a closer look will help us consider its impact here.

Gay/Queer Theatre?

Western theatre and theory is experiencing a shift from "gay and lesbian" to "queer" and *Angels in America* exemplifies that shift and its necessity. Here I want to emphasize that these plays are ideally most attractive to a gay population because of the themes and content. This is not to say that it does not have a wider appeal. Its queerness suggests it speaks to anyone who thinks about breaking out of a heterocentric existence.

Gay theatre has been around for long enough to have established a tradition for itself. Harvey Fierstein's *Torch Song Trilogy*, Alex Harding's *Only Heaven Knows*—one of the hits of the 1995 Sydney Mardi Gras—and the work of Gay Sweatshop might be seen to exemplify gay theatre. These plays contain characters who proudly identify themselves as homosexual and/or gay. They deal with themes of "coming out," and the trials of living within, and explicitly a part of, an often hostile heterosexual environment, within which we see conflict perhaps exemplified in bashings. Also expressed are the failed attempts to pin down relationships in a community that believes in sexual freedom. Another genre of gay plays are those dealing with AIDS. Larry Kramer's *The Normal Heart* might be said to typify this inherently political theatre movement. All of the above plays, whether dealing with problems of identity or more directly with HIV/AIDS, find a corresponding sense of pride, sexual identity, confrontation, politics and defiance. Yet whatever the plotlines of these plays it could be argued that they necessarily participate in opposition to a heterosexual hegemony.

Queer theory, as Bruce Parr suggests,

> celebrates sexual difference and invites participation in its diverse projects from all those opposed to heterosexism and homophobia. It strives to problematize rigid categories of gender and sexuality and highlights the illusory nature of identity and subjectivity. And much else. (Queer also encompasses issues of class, race, ethnicity and nation.) (28)

An example of queer theatre may be found in the work of Neil Bartlett, within the company Gloria. Bartlett's work for instance contains a gender fluidity such that actors play a particular gender to which their sex is not necessarily relevant. In Gloria's production of *Sarrasine*, three actors performed simultaneously the role of Zambinella, a famous castrato singer. These were a male counter-tenor, a female contralto, and Betty Bourne, a renowned British drag performer with a deep and gravelly voice.

Bartlett defines traditional gay theatre as "synonymous with the literary theatre—wordy, university-educated, un-physical, un-visual and tied to the authority of the author and director" (82). *Angels*' productions in Melbourne tended to elude this gay definition in terms of its fabulously visual nature. Bartlett uses it to signpost a road to certain change. *Angels in America* has a predominantly male cast of characters who would I think, in any re-production almost certainly need to be played by actors of a corresponding sex. It is difficult to imagine Prior, Belize, Louis or Roy Cohn being played by women playing homosexual men. The binding of sex and gender in *Angels* is necessary to the sexual politics of the play, giving it a "gay identity" polemic. Most of the male characters are seen to have varying degrees of homosexual preference. To retain a sense of credibility the actors playing these roles would need, because of the play's nudity, to be of the male sex. It is interesting to note then how Kushner specifies that the actress playing Hannah Pitt, should also play the Rabbi Isidor Chemelwitz and Henry, Cohn's male doctor. In the Melbourne production both the Rabbi and Henry, Martin Heller and the Bolshevik were played by William McClusky. In Sydney however, the casting of these roles followed Kushner's directive.

Angels in America's queerness is illustrated in its recognition of an America beset with problems of race, morality and religion that all try to control sexuality within a heterosexual ideal. *Angels* then looks forward to an alternative system as described by Belize, the black "ex-ex drag queen" who most closely epitomizes queer:

> And everyone in Balenciaga gowns with red corsages, and
> big dance palaces full of music and lights and racial impu-
> rity and gender confusion .... And all the deities are
> creole, mulatto, brown as the mouths of rivers ... Race,
> taste, and history finally overcome. (*Perestroika* 77–8)

The very nature of the production is explicit about its celebration of sexual, racial and national difference. All signification in *Angels* is set up relative to an American schema, a society of compulsory hetero-sexuality. The plays' epic emphasis on the need for change within the American nation, juxtaposing class, ethnicity and race show a nation out of control. Its non-linear narrative, the juxtaposition of circumstances through split scenes, the hallucination and fantasy and the chaos in heaven all demonstrate an uncontrollability that convinces me that *Angels in America* is very queer. Through characters like Roy Cohn, we see explicit heterosexism and homophobia, and its devastating implications, not only on the individual, but on those around him. His character is also critical in emphasizing the problems within identity politics.

Put all too simply, queer works for the liberal expression of desire. Desire, sexual or otherwise, is limited only by the imagination and the socialization of the desirer. It is not bound by notions of identity. Identity, being a politically rigid category, necessarily participates in, and consequently maintains and strengthens, the dominant discourse it would otherwise seek to change. It creates a polarity, is necessarily oppositional, and is consequently victimized and/or legitimized. Roy Cohn's interpretation of homosexual identity demonstrates how pliable identity is in powerful hands:

> Like all labels they tell you one thing and one thing only: where does an individual so identified fit in the food chain, in the pecking order? Not ideology, or sexual taste, but something much simpler: clout. Not who I fuck or who fucks me, but who will pick up the phone when I call, who owes me favours. This is what label refers to. Now to someone who does not understand this, homosexual is what I am because I have sex with men. But really this is wrong. Homosexuals are not men who sleep with other men. Homosexuals are men who in fifteen years of trying cannot get a pissant antidiscrimination bill through City Council. Homosexuals are men who know nobody and who nobody knows. Who have zero clout. Does this sound like me, Henry? (*Millennium Approaches* 45)

Cohn, homophobic and homosexual, illustrates a fundamental flaw in effective identity politics. Kushner's impressive creation of Cohn's acerbic personality illustrates the pressure on the individual to conform to a heterosexual matrix, same sex desires not withstanding.

It seems then that it is those against heterosexism to whom this play is speaking. It's saying, "Look! Look at what is happening in America, look how relatively ineffective our identity politics has been. This way of operating is just not working. We have to take a different strategy." The plays most certainly have a teleology which is queer. The fact that *Perestroika* is left open-ended suggests the door is left open for change. I think the signification of gay, and homosexual identity is wonderfully challenged here, and is worth deeper consideration.

Both American and Australian societies are controlled by the assumptions of a dominant heterosexuality; assumptions that are made clear by Adrian Kiernander's far-reaching definition of queer.

> ... queer is *not* necessarily connected with sexual prac-
> tices but, for example, anyone is at least a little bit queer
> who has ever, even for a moment, fantasized about the
> possibility of engaging in sexual activity which is not
> heterosexual, married, monogamous, procreative and in
> the missionary position.

Most of which is explicitly represented in the plays. *Angels* is seen to illustrate the ever present and needful concept of coming out, the conflict created through the binarism of sexuality, "homosexual" and "heterosexual" relationships, and most frankly AIDS. It also plays with a limited sense of gender and sex distinction, an ineffec-tuality of sexual identity, racial tension, class distinction, fantasy, imagination and "national themes." This epic presentation is both "gay" and "queer." These things do have a vital relevance in both the US and Australia, yet there are pronounced differences between the American and Australian experience.

America, Australia and AIDS

Angels in America concentrates the AIDS epidemic. Being taken into the hospital rooms and beds of those suffering from AIDS, and witnessing the dementia emphasized through the productions' magic realism is an alarming experience for gay men. The Melbourne Theatre Company programme gives a chronology of the epidemic from its recognition in the US in 1981, to November 1988 when the number of AIDS cases in America had reached over 100,000. This chronology also gives the American government's phlegmatic response to the crisis. This information emphasizes to an Australian audience the gravity of the situation Kushner writes about and the difference in relative experience. Inserted into these pages at relevant points are the corresponding Australian statistics on reported HIV cases and AIDS deaths which demonstrate another very different impact. It is certain that the response to the AIDS crisis from the Australian Labor government, newly elected in March 1983, was far more compassionate, less politically motivated, and more politically forward looking than that of the Reagan administration. Justice Michael Kirby makes clear the difference:

> Although there have been many failings, it is remarkable to think of the progress our country has made in explicit discussions of sexual transmission and in enlightened strategies to prevent contamination from infected drug equipment. In many ways, Australia's enlightenment led the world. What a contrast is our tale to that of the United States. President Reagan could not bring himself to mention the word AIDS for the first five years of his presidency, in an epicentre of the epidemic. (viii)

At this time under the direction of Neal Blewett, then federal Minister for Health, AIDS Councils at both federal and state levels were established. Following this initiative there was an almost unopposed bipartisan political stratagem which led in 1988 to a White Paper which Dennis Altman relates

> was produced by a committee headed by the Minister, and established two goals of AIDS policy as being "to eliminate transmission of the virus; and to minimize the personal and social impact of HIV infection." ... Commonwealth funding for the next three years, to rise from $42.4 million in 1988/9 to $94.5 million in 1992/93 ... (58)

Adam Carr tells us that the US has about six times the rate of infection per head of population than Australia. In reference to the containment of AIDS, he states "in bringing the spread of HIV ... under control ... Australia has achieved results much better than

those in the United States, and comparable with any in the world"
(17).

This information seems to demonstrate a remarkable attitude and
response by the Hawke government to the AIDS crisis. I am well
aware that thousands in Australia have felt the full impact of HIV/
AIDS. And if we have not been touched by personal loss, then our
lives have certainly been complicated especially in terms of the fear
associated with sexual practice. It is my contention, however, that
Australia *as a whole*, because of its action, has not felt the same
devastation enacted in *Angels in America*. A fact, at the risk of
sounding smug, of which we can be proud.

After a long line of AIDS plays produced in this country including
Larry Kramer's *The Normal Heart*, and at a time when the gay
community in particular has spent years enduring HIV/AIDS, within
ourselves, our partners, and our friends, many here have said that as
an "AIDS" play Angels in America did not attract the numbers it
deserved. One close friend who chose not to go at all may be
speaking for many in the gay community. He said that he was aware
of the graphic handling of HIV/AIDS in the play. He has had many
friends die, and having seen them in the most appalling states of ill
health and imminent death he did not want to be reminded in the
theatre of the ghastly progression of the disease. Consequently the
play failed to attract many who might otherwise identify very
strongly with it.

Angels in America as a feature of mainstream theatre, whilst
having a queer vision, enters into dominant discourse from a gay
perspective. Amazingly *Angels* limits itself because of its themes and
the bourgeois places in which it is produced. It is regrettable that a
play mounted by a state theatre company and found in these estab-
lishments can then be categorized as high art. I am certain in Melbourne it was not only aspects of the play that kept people away, but
the reputation of the company producing it. That is of producing
canonical texts. Politically this can be seen as advantageous. It introduces a queer agenda into the citadels of high art. But at what cost?
There is here the "tall poppy syndrome," a demonstrated antagonis-
tic public reaction to anything that makes itself taller than the
average. Americanism is well known for putting itself above the
many. Crusader Hillis makes a prophetic statement in his article
appearing prior to the opening of Melbourne's 1993 production:

Australians seem to enjoy lopping tall poppies and *Angels*, were it to have only adoring press here, could attract such a reaction.

It appears, it did.

There is little doubt that for many individuals these were difficult plays to understand. I had a casual "over the counter" conversation with a gay acquaintance working in a Melbourne cafe who saw both parts. He told me he felt completely bamboozled, lost and disappointed. He claimed he could not understand where the play was going and why it seemed to chop and change all the time. That is, he found the transition between reality and dream states confusing. *Angels* often takes a queer flight from realism. To some unfamiliar with performance, literary or critical theory, a non-linear narrative detracts from the realism they might expect. Confusion arises when one scene does not apparently follow from another. This would surely have compromised the productions' word-of-mouth publicity.

The emphasis on themes from a gay identified perspective inevitably relies heavily on a sympathetic community, one which is the most likely to understand the issues concerned and is more likely to appreciate the kinds of changes the plays advocate. Queer is specifically an "inyaface" position. *Angels in America* is a confrontational production. Despite and because of its dominance in the media over the last ten years, AIDS is still confronting. It signifies to many, whether we think it should or not, a conflation of homosexuality, disease and death. If *Angels* is also alienating its gay audience because of its graphic depiction of AIDS, then it is inevitable that it is going to suffer at the box office.

Angels does maintain an unavoidable exclusivity, despite its fantastic scope, because it is intellectual, queer and gay. It compromises another potent area of its forward looking queer agenda by excluding women, in particular lesbians. Its intellectuality seemed to inhibit its word-of-mouth advantage. Even then it alienated some Australian gays, arguably some of the people to whom it makes its political appeal, by embedding its argument in America and in HIV/AIDS.

It is a most peculiar fact that *Angels'* box office returns were much lower than might have been expected when we consider the quality of the play and the productions, and the media's enthusiastic response. In 1994, Stephen Dunne did some investigation into why gay men were not attending arts events set up during or by the Sydney Gay and Lesbian Mardi Gras:

> Overall, in a community that conservatively numbers at least 300,000 people, not including the OS visitors, the Mardi Gras-funded theatre festival managed total attendances of a little over 3,000 people. It's also clear that lesbian work has a much higher success rate than gay male work. ("Bums on Seats")

One has to note that this survey was done the year after *Angels in America* appeared in Sydney. It is stressed later in the article that "lesbian audiences were more loyal than gay men." And Campion Decent, a Mardi Gras board member is quoted in Dunne's article as saying:

> Is it that the boys just want sequins, laughter and muscle? And do we therefore give them sequins, laughter and muscle?

This may help explain some of the attendance figures.

Despite all of this we cannot underestimate its impact. Like Todd, the visiting Adonis, *Angels* has a definite attraction. Whether people saw it or not, it is legendary:

> Far more people are pretending to have seen this show than were actually there. (Dunne "Exuent")

It generated a great deal of media excitement, and who knows what impact it will have on Australia's theatre practitioners? As a piece of theatre it makes a masterful contribution to the discourse of queer which may in fact be its greatest offering to an Australia that is coming to terms with its own identity as a multicultural nation. Australia's transition to a republic makes it timely for our theatre practitioners to create a work as important and influential to Australia as *Angels* is to America.

Notes

1. The plays in the 1993 STC subscription season were: *Death and the Maiden* by Ariel Dorfman; *Dancing at Lughnasa* by Brian Friel; *Into the Woods*, music and lyrics by Stephen Sondheim, book by James Lapine; *Top Girls* by Caryl Churchill; *The Garden of Granddaughters* by Stephen Sewell; *Coriolanus* by William Shakespeare; *Summer of the Aliens* by Louis Nowra; *Brilliant Lies* by David Williamson; *The Rise and Fall of Little Voice* by Jim Cartwright; and *The Visit* by Friedrich Dürrenmatt, adapted by Maurice Valency.
2. These plays were: *Wednesday to Come* by Renée; *The Dutch Courtesan* by John Marston; and *Faust* by Goethe.
3. These plays were: *The Sisters Rosensweig* by Wendy Wasserstein; *Hysteria* by Terry Johnson; and *The Shaughraun* by Dion Boucicault.
4. Letter of May 25, 1995. Other shows in the season were: Accidental Death of An Anarchist* by Dario Fo; *Crow* by Louis Nowra; *Morning Sacrifice* by Dymphna Cusak; *A Little Like Drowning* by Anthony Minghella; *The Emerald Room* by Dennis Watkins and Chris Harriott; *The Swan* by Elizabeth Egloff; and *Warsaw Tango* by Teatro del Sur (Argentina).
5. *Sydney Morning Herald* Wednesday, May 10, 1995, page 17.

Works Cited

Altman, Dennis. "The Most Political of Diseases." *Aids in Australia*. Eds. Eric Timewell, Victor Minichiello, David Plummer. Sydney: Prentice Hall, 1992. 55–72.

Bartlett, Neil. "Preface." *A Vision of Love Revealed in Sleep. Gay Plays: Volume Four*. Ed. Michael Wilcox. London: Methuen Drama, 1990. 82–4.

Bloch, Felicity. "Compelling drama as AIDS strikes." *The Australian Jewish News* (29 October 1993): 6.

—————. "Award-winning *Angels in America*." *The Australian Jewish News* (16 September 1994): 28.

Carr, Adam. "What is AIDS?" *Aids in Australia*. Eds. Eric Timewell, Victor Minichiello, David Plummer. Sydney: Prentice Hall, 1992. 3–23.

Dunne, Stephen. "Astounding Angels." *Sydney Star Observer* (5 March 1993): 14.

——————. "Exuent, Pursued by Realism." *Sydney Star Observer* (22 December 1993): 37.

——————. "Bums on seats." *Sydney Star Observer* (8 April 1994): 15.

Hillis, Crusader. "Making angels fly." *Melbourne Star Observer* (15 October 1993): 11.

——————. "Introduction." *Melbourne Star Observer* (19 August 1994): 22.

Kiernander, Adrian. *Sic Transit Gloria: A draft genealogy of queer theatre/theory*. Publication forthcoming.

Kirby, Michael. "Forward." *Aids in Australia*. Eds. Eric Timewell, Victor Minichiello, David Plummer. Sydney: Prentice Hall, 1992. vii–ix.

Kushner, Tony. *Angels in America, Part One: Millennium Approaches*. New York: Theatre Communications Group, 1992, 1993.

——————. *Angels in America, Part Two: Perestroika*. New York: Theatre Communications Group, 1992, 1994.

Lane, Laurie. "Hope." *Brother Sister* (9 September 1994): 21.

Larkin, John. "Descent of a darker angel." *The Sunday Age* (Melbourne: 24 October 1993): 'Agenda' section.

——————. "Land of the Free, Home of the Scared." *The Sunday Age* (Melbourne: 11 September 1994): 7.

Neill, Rosemary. "Dazzling, visionary drama." *The Australian* (22 February 1993): 2.

Olb, Suzanne. *"Angels in America." Stages* (September 1994): 35.

Parr, Bruce. *But is it queer? Defining Australian Gay and Lesbian Playwrighting*. Conference paper delivered at the Australasian Drama Studies Association, Adelaide, 1994.

Phillips, Bill. *"Angels in America Part One: Millennium Approaches." Adelaide Gay Times* (7 October 1994): 22.

——————. *"Angels in America Parts 1 & 2*: An address on gay theatre, a personal reflection." Paper given to the Adelaide Uranian Society, 31 October 1994.

——————. *"Principally, a comedy … Angels in America Part 2: Perestroika." Adelaide Gay Times* (4 November 1994): 22.

Radic, Leonard. "Powerful and provocative punch." *The Age* (Melbourne: 21 October 1993): 19.

Romney, Jason. "Prophets of doom." *Melbourne Herald Sun* (5 September, 1994): 59.

Schofield, Leo. "Leo at Large." *Sydney Morning Herald* (13 February 1993): 26.

——————. "Leo at Large." *Sydney Morning Herald* (27 February 1993): 26.

Sydney Morning Herald (10 May 1995): 17.

Sydney Theatre Company. "Plays and Performances." *Sydney Theatre Company fifteenth annual report.* Sydney Theatre Company: 1993.

Thomson, Helen. "*Angels in America, King Lear*" *The Australian* (22 October 1993): 10.

Williams, Geoffrey. "Theatre." *Brother Sister* (5 November 1993): 16.

Acknowledgements

I would like to gratefully acknowledge the assistance of the following people:

Peter Eckersall, Adrian Kiernander, Ian McDonald, Bruce Parr, David Pledger, Jill Smith, Joanne Tompkins, Bill Wilson, Stephen, Shane, Brace, David and Bradley. The cast and crew of the NOT YET IT'S DIFFICULT Company's production of *Taking Tiger Mountain by Strategy* inside which I performed earlier drafts of this essay.

"How Like an Angel
Came I Down!"

by Patrick Friesen

Nicki van Tempelhoff and Zazie de Paris in
Engel in America. Photo © Matthias Horn.

"How Like an Angel Came I Down!"

by Patrick Friesen

I love the ending. I wish I'd written it. It seems obvious enough now, like it's been done somewhere before. Maybe it has. The nerve of it. Thinking of the ceiling in a stage play. Balconies, ladders, stairs, yes. But a ceiling? Another wall. A wall to heaven. And heaven, or outer space, taken so naturalistically.

I love this ending. Seeing it, hearing it, the sheer physicality of it in the Walter Kerr Theatre. A moment with incredible resonances for the senses and the imagination. A moment to take off on.

"How like an angel came I down!"

An ending that speaks at once of release, salvation, death, prophecy, and the endless opening up of human possibility, transcendence. An ending that speaks of birth.

Angels in America, a visitation from another sphere, another kind of power than Americans are accustomed to. Avenging angel, or stern, an embracing angel. But it's not one angel in the title, it's angels. Battalions of them, like UFOs. Blue Angels, maybe, like some acrobatic Air Force squadron of jet fighters. Guardian angels, holding hands, the blue ring of the ozone layer.

Or, more likely, angels inherent, a birthing, the becoming of angels.

"How like an angel came I down!"

PATRICK FRIESEN is a Winnipeg poet, playwright and filmmaker. His most recent play is *The Raft*, produced by Prairie Theatre Exchange in Winnipeg and Theatre & Co. in Kitchener. *Blasphemer's Wheel: Selected and New Poems* won the McNally Robinson Manitoba Book of the Year Award for 1994.

The play is about limits. The limits of humanity, its ultimate powerlessness in the face of nature. Disease and death as nature's great levellers.

Roy Cohn, with all his politics and telephones, with venereal warts up his ass. He squirms over semantics, sociological hierarchies, and power politics, but he can't escape his human vulnerability. Though he hides it under a barrage of obscenity and power brokerage.

A priggish church; the vulgar offices of its power. How it binds the individual in its community and in the rigidity of its doctrine. How it judges and condemns precisely what is most human.

The lonely, violent park bench. The desperate couch.

You can almost hear Joe's skeleton clatter. So little flesh on him, so little give and take. His whole being bent toward the squeaky-clean machine someone else decreed as model. The unbearable pressure of that.

Paralleled by the skinniness of Prior. Physical and spiritual starvations. Prior and Joe. Harper's dreams of snow. Her despair, her valium, her yearning for another world. She knows everything is collapsing, "systems of defense giving way" (17).

And the angel plummeting into the dying man's bedroom. Music and celestial light. Smoke and rending. The ceiling breaking open.

Divine intervention or human transcendence. Are they two different concepts? Or, simply, two namings of the same experience? God's hand reaching down; human arms rising. Prayer and answer, supplication and comfort.

"How like an angel came I down!" wrote Thomas Traherne in the 17th century.

"I that so long
Was nothing from eternity ... "

The angel as child within us. The child, as yet uncorrupted by culture, all its agents. The angel as human deity.

Prior has been told by a beautiful voice to look up. A grey feather has floated down to him. Is this what he is to look for? His own purity, the wisdom of his own long-forgotten divinity? The innate goodness of human beings?

Does an obscenity like Cohn hold a child inside? Is it possible to be so corrupted, so broken down, the child is destroyed? This is the question of salvation and redemption. And is there a way back?

The Christian doctrine of original sin made human. We are born, corrupted, and can be redeemed, not through intrusion from outside somewhere, but through a return to the innocence of infancy. Individual, self-contained redemption; heaven inherent in us.

Prior is each of us. He has been prior and will be again. The wheel turning; the repeating process of birth, earthly fall, death, and birth again. Nature, and the human construction banging into nature, is the fall. As if we are from two different sources; as if we are not part of nature.

Prior and his disease. Not a disease of culture, though it takes cultural forms. Disease is always natural. Only its forms keep shifting. Disease is opportunistic; it takes what is given, sex, religion, pollution, antibiotics, whatever, and does nature's work.

Whoever, whatever, we want to blame for any given disease is irrelevant. Such a strange human activity, pointing fingers amongst ourselves, to find a scapegoat on whom to hang the blame. What better villain than the victim?

"He's sick; he must have done something to deserve it." The summoners speak.

The voice of ideology. That kind of rigidity, the overlaying of some mental, ideal construct upon the flesh and blood man and woman breathing, eating, defecating, loving, and dying.

We die. That's it. Nature.

We all die. Do we deserve it? Does that make any sense? A kind of value system attached to disease and death; degrees of guilt, fine shadings of judgement. Elaborate grids of faith and belief to proclaim eternal life.

We can live and die as angels. Or, not. Is that what we mean by freedom?

Human culture recognizing its foundation, the wheel of nature, and choosing to build goodness, compassion and dignity upon that ground. Not the freedom away from something, but a freedom toward; the freedom to be rooted, as a tree, or as a bird is held by sky.

There is something comic here, as well. The angel does not pass lightly through the roof; nothing ghostly, no transformation, no osmosis. The angel is heavily physical, crashing through plaster and lathework. A clumsiness, slapstick even. Prior, hearing the music, seeing the lightshow, gives the event a humorous cultural framework.

"God almighty ... *Very* Stephen Spielberg" (118).

The effervescence of American culture meeting eternal verities.

And that distance in Prior, the contemporary American man. That capacity, that need, to diminish what is serious, even final. A postmodern sabotage; a fear; the decision to not face the hollow within, the angel banished, but to project this emptiness onto the world, and announce the world desolate and void of meaning.

This is not comedy as relief, but comedy as despair. It's a tightening of the screws; a rejection of nature, and a full embrace of culture.

> Greetings, Prophet;
> The Great Work begins:
> The Messenger has arrived. (119)

Whose messenger? Messenger of what news? And, what is the Great Work?

Nature has sent innumerable messages through its workings. Humans have seen nature's work, nature's responses to human greed, human arrogance and ignorance. Nature, without intentions, carries on. We see and learn, or we don't. No matter; nature is relentless.

We only see the message in forms our imagination is taught to read. Divine intervention. The metaphor of divinity; our imaginative construct for what we don't accept in nature, what we attribute to some Higher Being.

Yes, this could be an angel from heaven. Yes, it could be what we want to see. What we fear, and what we hope for. The intervention, the inevitability of nature, turning around human gall. The celestial event that holds the mystery, giving us an out.

As Prior says to Harper: "I usually say, 'Fuck the truth,' but mostly, the truth fucks you" (34). The truths of nature, and the truths of human experience as built up through time.

The angel delivers a message of apocalypse to Prior. In his disease, Prior embodies the prophecy, the Great Work of decimation. Earlier Prior has told his departing lover, Louis, a story of an early ancestor. A ship's captain, this ancestor went down in a winter storm near Nova Scotia. Seventy survivors, mostly women and children, rode in a leaky longboat. Each time the water rose too high in the boat, the crew members would grab the nearest passengers and hurl them out into the cold ocean. Until the ballast was right again. By the time the boat arrived in Halifax, nine of the original seventy people remained.

PRIOR: I think about that story a lot now. People in a
boat, waiting, terrified, while implacable, unsmiling
men, irresistably strong, seize ... maybe the person next
to you, maybe you, and with no warning at all, with
time only for a quick intake of air you are pitched into
freezing, turbulent water and salt and darkness to
drown. (42)

The lesson is obvious. The sacrifice of the most vulnerable so the
strong will survive. Contemporary society, its dominant members,
and those suffering from AIDS. In Prior's case, even his lover, deserts
him. The ruthless business of survival.

This story is central to the play. This is how the apocalypse
happens. This is the thinning out of society, the Darwinian proce-
dure.

The angel crashing through the ceiling. The messenger from afar.
An alien, an angel. Doom and the end of things, apocalypse. And the
opening up of the sky. The possibility of transcendence.

Prior, at the end of his story, admits that he is drawn to Louis'
cosmology, Louis' escape from the hard facts, and yet finds this
escape a ducking of responsibility.

"While time is running out I find myself drawn to anything that's
suspended, that lacks an ending—but it seems to me that it lets you
off scot-free" (42).

The angel is suspended above the world of this play until the very
end. The sound of distant wings, a beautiful voice speaking to Prior,
a grey feather floating down from the ceiling, foreshadow the
epiphany.

Suspension; the possibility of redemption, and also a finality. Fear
and hope. What is this hanging above us? These mighty wings. Will
they mean oblivion or rapture?

Louis, Cohn, and others, curse and run, anything to avoid the
angel's moment. Running from themselves?

Does each human have his or her own angel? The angel we see, is
this Prior's guardian? If so, is this the end version of the angel within
each person at birth? Is this personal redemption? The angel, so long
estranged, returning with a vengeance; an angel of doom which, yet,
is also the angel of redemption.

The angel's return.

The Great Work beginning. The Work of transformation. For Prior, shifting from flesh into nothing, or can one say, into Spirit? For American society, for the world, a parallel physical transformation, but also, possibly, a transformation into social tolerance and compassion.

The great wheel turning. The arrivals and departures of the angel, of the angels. Each human, in moments of transcendence. Redeemed, not by disease, but by an acceptance of disease, the non-judgement of disease, and so, a compassion that places each being in nature.

The promised voice, the beautiful voice of the angel, whispering to us in moments of despair. Whispering us toward the day of decisions, a hard day, a day of clarity, but also the day of the dove. The spirit awakened in each being, the flesh animated.

The Great Work is the transformation of men and women from the rigid tyranny of culture, what Traherne called custom, into the angels they all are.

So the angel plunges into a person's life. Not a symbol, nor a metaphor, but an angel. Bones, wings and ligaments. Breath, and then a voice. That's all, a divinity on earth.

Works Cited

Kushner, Tony. *Angels in America Part One: Millenium Approaches.* New York: Theatre Communications Group, 1994.

The Obscene Paradox

by Graham Dixon

Barbara Nusse, Matthias Fuchs, and Monica Bleiftsen
in *Engel in America*. Photo © Matthias Horn.

The Obscene Paradox:
Hope and Despair in *Angels in America*

by Graham Dixon

1. AIDS as a Three-Dimensional Saviour on a Two-Dimensional World of Baudrillardian Hyper-reality in Part One

Imagine a play with no protagonist. The action proceeds, some characters suffer unimaginably and die: others are left bereft, crazed, numb with shock. The performance goes on: lasting days, months, years. Uncounted numbers participate ...   —Elizabeth Osborne (1990)

The schizo is bereft of every scene, open to everything in spite of himself, living in the greatest confusion. He is himself obscene, the obscene play of the world's obscenity ... he can no longer produce himself as mirror. He is now only pure screen, a switching centre for all the networks of influence.   —Jean Baudrillard (1983)

GRAHAM DIXON is a Doctoral Candidate in Theatre at the University of California at Berkeley. His dissertation is titled "The Play(s) of AIDS," it deals with the existence of AIDS within theatrical plays and also within the Play of Society as a whole. He has published articles on *Angels in America* and John Osborne, with articles on homelessness and *Schindler's List* forthcoming. He is an actor, director and playwright.

> Ain't no angel gonna greet me,
> It's just you and I my friend.
> —Bruce Springsteen (1993)

We suffer in a world of paradox. An obscene paradox. The "play" in which we are walk-on characters contrasts with the "confusion" of Baudrillard's postmodern vision. In a world of uncertainty, a world in which the boundaries between what is "real" and what is "unreal" become increasingly dubious, hazy and even irrelevant, the spectre of AIDS rises with the inscrutable certainty of Hamlet's father. Remember me, Death whispers. The Western world was starting to forget about death: the old infectious diseases were fading memories, one died of luxury or old age. There is little tragic about the death of an eighty year-old in her sleep. But now Tragedy reappears, reasserts itself as young men and women die an often terrible death. The modern doctor stands as helpless as Oedipus watching his Thebes slowly rot and die. Perversely, the unexpected revival of a tragic disease has injected life into old representational forms which had begun to eye themselves suspiciously in the mirror, a process which seemed to be inevitably leading to their destruction. While AIDS disintegrates the bodies of those it afflicts, it has apparently reintegrated the representational forms of modernism, or at least offered them new material to argue their relevance. *Angels in America* won the Pulitzer Prize and many Tonys, it sold out on Broadway and in the West End ... AIDS plays are now a mainstream spectacle of modern theatrical endeavour.

Before tackling the multi-dimensional complexities of *Angels in America* I shall construct a conceptual framework. Like Edmund Husserl in *Logical Investigations*, I argue that we should return to the "things themselves," the "things" in our case being the "Janus-faced thing" which Bert States speaks of in *Great Reckonings in Little Rooms*: "the sign/image." The sign/image is the dramatic play, but the play involves the "play" of Baudrillard's shifting kaleidoscope of seductive appearance. The pre-AIDS artistic sign, as part of the traditional representational model, has difficulty existing at all. For in the postmodern world there may not be a "thing" to say anything about. As Baudrillard suggests in "The Ecstasy of Communication":

> The scene and the mirror no longer exist; instead there is
> a screen and network. In place of the reflexive transcend-
> ence of mirror and scene, there is a non-reflecting surface,

> an immanent surface where operations unfold—the
> smooth operational surface of communication. (126)

In the postmodern structure there is an eternal unfolding of images replicating one another without any need of an original—we languish in a Barthean flow of endless commutability. It is the play of these imagistic simulacrums that I shall consider in *Angels in America*. Baudrillard originally argued that the constant commutability was an inevitable process, both unstoppable and irreversible; but AIDS has brought about a remarkable conceptual transformation. In *The Transparency of Evil*, Baudrillard has recently suggested that "the sudden whirlpools which we dub catastrophes are really the thing that saves us from catastrophe," and continues with what might initially seem a perverse evaluation:

> So the actual catastrophe may turn out to be a carefully
> modulated strategy of our species—or more precisely, *our
> viruses*, our extreme phenomena, which are definitely
> real, albeit localized, may be what allows us to preserve
> the energy of that virtual catastrophe which is the motor
> of all our processes, whether economic or political, artis-
> tic or historical. [My emphasis.] (69)

To be succinct: AIDS is a saviour. The "virtual catastrophe" implies the reappearance of the world of three-dimensional reality, related to an escape from the smooth surface of hyper-reality. AIDS is a brutal reality in a world otherwise made up of hyper-reality, it provides a third dimension, a height above the surface from which we may identify previously hidden features. AIDS is a unique societal Sword of Damocles—paradoxically, it saves while it destroys, destroys while it saves. I will consider whether the artistic and commercial success of *Angels in America* may be traced to its being held captive on the Baudrillardian surface or whether it originates in a successful rise above it. Ultimately, this leads to a consideration of whether Baudrillard's contention of AIDS-as-saviour has any validity beyond an admittedly fascinating intellectual licentiousness. *Angels in America* shall be the mirror (screen) for this study.

The dominant feature of most of the characters' lives in *Angels in America, Part One* (hereafter *AA1*) is "chaos." The following ex-change appears early in the play:

ROY: Crazy life.

> JOE: Chaotic.
> ROY: Well, but God bless chaos. Right?
> JOE: Ummm ... (15)

Roy's desk, with its constantly noisy and elaborate phone system, is the perfect image of this "chaos." This "chaos" is defined according to the layman's tradition. We will move onto Chaos (in the sense of Chaos Theory) later, but for now all is merely disconnected, fragmented, illogical. While there is instant communication there is little understanding: conversations are started but never finished as they are interrupted by others which are in turn curtailed in an endless cycle of confusion. While Roy's overt sexuality is subsumed beneath a layer of self-righteous denial, Kushner tells us that he "*conducts business with great energy, impatience and sensual abandon*" (11). Roy is in love with chaos, he is in love with the avoidance of genuine communication that the phone system enables. He touches the phone with the selfish abandon with which he touches his lovers. Roy's ability to float easily in the hyper-reality of postmodern communication also enables him to indulge in a form of sophistic verbal materialism later in the play, as he denies that he is a homosexual because "what I am is defined entirely by who I am ... Roy Cohn is a heterosexual man, Henry, who fucks around with guys" (45). Words have no concrete meaning, they drift with Roy in the postmodern ether. Frank Rich suggests that *AA1* is "a searching and radical rethinking of American political drama"(29), and in Roy's adherence to a paradigm normally associated with the Left we can identify the basic framework of this rethinking. The endless signification and lack of certain semantic meaning of words implied by poststructuralist theory in general, and deconstruction in particular, almost always implies the dismantling of Western Reason and the Conservative institutions which it engenders and which nurture it. Roy is at the centre of these institutions, he can, after all, get the President's wife on the phone within fifteen minutes; but the centre now uses the shifting paradigms of those who would challenge its power to preserve its position—Roy can define himself as not being something which he clearly is because words are merely improvisational tools in a bricoleur design. The Right elegantly appropriates the weapons of the Left.

Harper is in direct juxtaposition to Roy. We first see her in scene three, immediately after Roy's frenetic introduction. Harper is sitting alone at home, listening to the radio: immobile, lonely, alienated from Roy's system. Ironically, it is Harper who understands the Janus-faced nature, the fragility of the system that Roy, the practically successful man-of-the-world, holds in such awe:

> HARPER: People are lonely, people left alone, sit talking nonsense to the air, imagining ... beautiful systems dying, old fixed orders spiralling apart ... (16)

Roy's talking to numerous people on the phone is "talking nonsense to the air" according to Harper and she sees this as just another example of a world rapidly losing any coherence. She goes on to describe the Ozone layer as "a kind of gift from God," and sees its destruction as both a catalyst for, and symbol of, the destruction of the systems that had previously protected humanity. At this early point in *AA1* Roy *appears* in power while Harper *appears* powerless. The two positions are laid out side by side with a deceptive simplicity, the view is muddied by the appearance of a strange new virus.

AIDS appears with neither a bang nor a whimper, but in the guise of a simple, compelling *pause*:

> PRIOR: Cats know when something's wrong.
> LOUIS: Only when you stop feeding them.
> PRIOR: They know. That's why Sheba left, because she knew.
> LOUIS: Knew what?
> (*Pause.*) (20)

AIDS is soon turned into a joke with Prior's punning on the word "lesion," a tendency of avoidance which soon becomes a pattern. While on the one hand Kushner glorifies in the sheer beauty of spoken language (and in his indubitable talent at creating it) he also sees language in a more problematic, darker, almost Pinteresque manner. *AA1* is perhaps far removed from the Comedies of Menace, but in the constant attempts at humorous avoidance we can see what Pinter defines as the "constant stratagem to cover nakedness ... I think we communicate only too well, in our silence, in what is unsaid, and that what takes place is continual evasion, desperate rearguard attempts to keep ourselves to ourselves"(39). One might consider Roy's frantic telephone calls in this light, as well as Harper's lonely ruminations; and also Louis, as he tries to explain why he may have to leave Prior. Initially he hides behind the pseudo-intellectual

explanation that "maybe a person who has this neo-Hegelian positiv-
ist sense of constant historical progress towards happiness or
perfection ... can't incorporate sickness into his sense of how things
are meant to go ...," but he soon admits to more frightening concerns: "Maybe vomit ... and sores and disease ... really frighten him"
(25). Louis's "stratagem" is to hide behind the comfy distance of the
intellect; but the intellectual explanation soon fades into the terrible
physicality of AIDS. At first Kushner avoids dwelling on this physical
reality; it is hinted at by the characters and then drawn away from—
AIDS is glanced at briefly rather than carefully examined.

These brief glances are part of an overall pattern of fragmentation
in the play. The split scene device encapsulates this fragmentation, it
brings a confused lucidity to the complex transformations and
juxtapositions of time and place which embody the Baudrillardian
"immanent surface." Scene 7 clearly illustrates how Kushner
enlightens through staying just on the comprehensible side of the
line between utter confusion and understanding. As he says in the
stage directions, "*for some reason, Prior has appeared in this one. Or
Harper has appeared in Prior's dream. It is bewildering.*" But there is a
method to this bewilderment:

> (*Harper appears.*)
> HARPER: Are you ... who are you?
> PRIOR: Who are you?
> HARPER: What are you doing in my hallucination?
> PRIOR: I'm not in your hallucination. You're in
> my dream. (31)

Here is a surface in which "operations" may indeed "unfold" without
normal constructions of time and place. It is clearly immanent, it
exists within the minds of the protagonists without any coherence in
the physical world. Each knows they are dreaming/hallucinating—
Kushner produces an ironic mixture of Brechtian objectivity and
alienation with the dizzying onslaught of hyper-real sensation. The
Voice interrupts this confusing, but luscious mixture; Harper has
just spoken of the "threshold of revelation" (34) but the revelation is
merely a confused suggestion from the Voice to "look up" (34)
followed by the less-than-enlightening statement that "a breath in
air" is "floating down," ending with

> VOICE: Glory to ...
> (*Silence.*) (35)

The Voice's "*silence*" correlates with Prior's "*pause;*" Prior soon admits he has AIDS while at this point we cannot know whether the Voice's "*silence*" is merely because she has nothing more to say or whether what she has to say is too terrible to speak all at once. As we shall see later, the two possibilities may not be as dualistically opposed as we might think.

The method to the split scene device materializes when one half of a scene ironically comments upon and reflects the other half. In one of the most consummate examples of the technique (act two, scene 4), Kushner places Joe and Roy in a "*fancy straight bar*" while Louis and a Man are in Central Park. The superficially polite but wonderfully vicious platitudes of the bar conversation contrast hilariously with the strangely unaroused sexuality of the park pick-up. The conversations meet:

> JOE: Can't Washington wait?
> ROY: You do what you need to do, Joe. What *you* need. You. Let her life go where it wants to go. You'll both be better for that. *Somebody* should get what they want.
> MAN: What do you want?
> LOUIS: I want you to fuck me, hurt me, make me bleed. (54)

AIDS is the common background to all of this: our knowledge of Roy's condition and his reluctance to accept it ironize his aphoristic advice, while Louis's apparent disregard for the risks of contracting AIDS provide an image of another form of denial. Resolute action is impossible in this world—Louis and the Man indulge in an attempt at S/M role-playing, but it breaks down as Louis admits that his "lover doesn't know" while the Man reveals that he still "lives with his parents" (!) (55). The echo of a simpler time in the past when role-playing came so easily becomes a sad grotesque, a reminder that sexual fulfilment in itself is now a fantasy. The Man doesn't want to use a condom, Louis nearly leaves because of it, but they end up fucking anyway, only to have the rubber break and the sex prematurely ended ... real sex is diminished, fragmented and eventually destroyed. AIDS is the framework on which Kushner builds his bricoleur design of this destruction and denial: he never allows the audience to focus on any one type for long, each simply "appears" much as Harper "appears" in Prior's hallucination. The audience catches a brief glance of the type, but never for long enough to rationalize it, to set it within a coherent, logical conceptual design. This facet of the play may be viewed in several ways. On one level, the device makes for a highly entertaining evening, simply contrasting/combining realistic dialogue with fantastical, almost circus-like technique. Kushner is also avoiding the kind of dogmatic, step-by-step political diatribe of other AIDS plays (*The Normal Heart*, et al.). For our purposes the technique shows how Kushner may agree with Baudrillard's contention that "the screen and the mirror no longer exist," *Angels in America* does not mirror the world as much as it produces a fragmented impression of it. On the smooth surface of communication no idea, statement or action stays still long enough to become a rational whole. All is, as Roy suggests, chaos.

The chaos of the split scenes develops until it merges in a kind of choric lament to the betrayals and inconsistencies of postmodern life. Each character hauntingly echoes the other, each encapsulates and defines the other's loneliness:

> HARPER: Oh God. Home. The moment of truth has arrived.
> JOE: Harper.
> LOUIS: I'm going to move out.
> PRIOR: The fuck you are.
> JOE: Harper. Please listen. I still love you very much. You're still my best buddy. I'm not going to leave you.
> (76)

Kushner suggests that "*the proceedings may be a little confusing but not the final results*," a comment which might suffice for the whole second act of the play, as it becomes increasingly embroiled in a hallucinatory environment in which the past invades the present. The voices on the real and immanent surfaces are indeed confused, but what of the (V)oice from above? The Voice of Death, the Angel … whatever it is, is indelibly linked with the Voice of AIDS. It comes from above both in the physical space of the theatre and, perhaps, in the theoretical modality of Baudrillard's theory. So the development of the Voice's influence, culminating in the appearance of the Angel at the end of *AA1* is vital in our evaluation of whether the "virtual catastrophe" of AIDS is indeed a three-dimensional saviour. The Voice is hardly enlightening, it is rather confusing:

> VOICE: No death, no; A marvellous work and a wonder
> we undertake, an edifice awry we sink and straighten, a
> great Lie we abolish, a great error we correct, with the
> rule, sword and broom of Truth!
> PRIOR: What are you talking about, I ...
> VOICE: I am on my way; when I am manifest, our work
> begins: Prepare for the parting of the air, The breath,
> the ascent, Glory to ... (62)

What *is* she talking about? Is the Voice merely a kind of *reductio ad absurdum* of religious rhetoric? She seems to offer "hope" with "no death," but the description of what she actually is offering is too amorphous and imprecise to engender much confidence in the seriously ill Prior. The Voice is all style and little substance; it is cut off in mid sentence to be replaced by Martin's political platitudes in the next scene much as Roy's clients were cut off in his opening scene. Indeed, the process seems just as easy whether one is indulging in apparently meaningless small talk or whether one is delivering a Saving Message: all forms of communication are fleeting and constantly threatened with arbitrary cessation. A humorous, lightly sardonic tone characterizes these lightning changes of perspective, as when the "*great book*" appears in act two, scene 2 in "*an astonishing blaze of light*" with "*a huge chord wounded by a gigantic choir*"—a sequence of events which is completely unnoticed by one of the characters on the stage at the time. Uncertainty and apparent chaos are the key ingredients here, and the Angel, far from providing the respite that she promises, is an integral part of the pattern. Louis expounds a possible explanation for the fluid, immanent surface which increasingly dominates the play:

> LOUIS: ... there are no gods here, no ghosts and spirits in
> America, there are no angels in America, no spiritual
> past, no racial past, there's only the political, and the
> decoys and the ploys to manoeuvre around the inescap-
> able battle of politics, the shifting downwards and
> outwards of political power to the people ... (92)

There are "no angels in America" and yet, paradoxically, we are watching *Angels in America*.

Two vital questions arise: (1) Is the Angel some kind of postmodern Godot for whom the characters wait in a kind of eternally unfolding stasis? (2) If "there's only the political," what precisely *is* political in this world of constant ebb and flow. First, there clearly *are* angels in this world, and there are also spirits and ghosts: Prior is haunted by several ancestors and even Ethel Rosenberg makes a brief but vital appearance. The ghosts become, in a sense, more "real" (or at least more vivacious) than the characters they miraculously appear before. Roy and Prior are dying of AIDS, inexorably shrinking and descending towards death; the ghosts surprise them, stride into the "real" world and diffuse their hallucinatory energy around them. Louis's political assertions are suspect as well: Roy is the archetypal political animal, yet his posturing, dealing and lying do not save him from either the New York Bar Association or ultimately from AIDS. Politics, that art of the possible, is rendered impotent by a world in which, paradoxically, everything is possible (ghosts appearing, angels descending, mutual dreams) and yet also nothing is possible as AIDS, betrayal and the stultifying anomie of the postmodern world reduce the characters to endlessly repetitive cycles of despair.

Oddly enough, it is Harper, the apparently impotent and hapless housewife at the beginning of the play who finds some sort of fulfilment in the saccharine world of Mr. Lies at the end. She may be blissfully unaware but she is, at least, blissful. She escapes the despair through becoming an integral part of it, through ceasing to struggle with philosophical and political questions which are unanswerable and thus irrelevant. In a supreme irony, she lives up to Roy's dictum to "live in the raw wind, naked, alone" (58), one which he vainly aspires to himself. But Harper's triumph is perhaps Quixotic—she is naked and alone in a National Geographic world, a world in which desolation is perfect, in which one may indeed "respect the delicate ecology" of one's "delusions." She escapes one area of the immanent surface only to be entrapped on another ... Mr. Lies offers precisely what his name implies.

The old truism has it that birth, death and copulation are the only certainties of life, but the end of *AA1* suggests that even these fail to rise above the immanent surface. Prior's state at the end of the play is essentially an amalgam of all three experiences. He is captured by "*an intense sexual feeling*" as both death (apparently) and the Angel approach. Now, as sexuality and fever draw him towards death and an apparently positive rebirth, now one might expect the play to rise above the surface, to provide evidence that AIDS might indeed be a form of perverse saviour as it forces humanity to consider itself in brutal three-dimensionality.

But what does the trumpet sound? What is Prior's reaction to this unique, potentially enlightening revelation?

The answer:

> (*an awestruck whisper*) God almighty ...
> *Very* Steven Spielberg. (118)

The Angel arrives in suitably breathtaking manner, but it is merely an illusory splendour—the play ends as the Great Work begins, a Work which involves a blackout and the breaking of the theatrical illusion. The "virtual catastrophe" of AIDS does not save us from anything, it does not raise us above the smooth surface, for in all its tragic intensity it is merely part of the surface. The reality of Prior's suffering is submerged by the pervasive immanence of a Spielbergian/Baudrillardian hyper-reality. This immanence is a block to any restoration of the "energy" which Baudrillard identifies as essential to human activity—throughout the play characters are left in stasis while magical special effects and their attendant ghosts flow freely around them. So Ethel Rosenberg magically appears to taunt Roy in his agony before miraculously vanishing: it is the Angel who descends with all the ephemeral nature and splendour of modern special effects as Prior remains still. AIDS is not a "virtual catastrophe," but rather it serves to accentuate the inability of the characters to effectively influence their own lives.

The ineffective stasis of "reality" contrasts with the effective fluidity of hyper-reality:

> ROY: I'm immortal, Ethel. (*He forces himself to stand.*) I
> have forced myself into history. I ain't never gonna die.
> ETHEL ROSENBERG: (*A little laugh, then,*) History is
> about to crack wide open. Millennium approaches.
> (112)

The rational world of cause and effect, a world in which "history" exists, which can be "forced" into, the world which Roy must believe in because he both defines it and is defined by it, this world is cast aside with the delicate, omnipotent ease of Ethel's "*little laugh.*" Ethel, a victim of the politics of a supposedly rational world is a suitable herald for the coming of a brave, but terrible new world.

What do we find when history cracks open? Not the terrible yet cozy stability of Baudrillard's AIDS-as-virtual-catastrophe-yet-saviour ... but rather a yawning, ever widening chasm which allows an uninhibited flood of hyper-reality. *Angels in America* would be "complete" with the ending of Part One: hyper-reality is left to flow uninhibited and all humanity is left to do is to swim or drown in its stream. With *Angels in America, Part Two* (hereafter *AA2*) Kushner examines the plight of characters attempting to survive in hyper-reality. He considers whether we can draw back from the brink, stem the flow of deconstructive hyper-reality and thus restore the boundaries of the individual in his/her search for self-fulfilment.

2. When History Cracks Open—Man as the AIDS of the Universe and the Restructuring of Chaos in Part Two

> Shedding one's skin: the snake that cannot shed its skin perishes. So do the spirits who are prevented from chang-ing their opinions; they cease to be spirit.
>
> —Fredrich Nietzsche

In the playwright's notes to *AA2* Kushner states that "*Perestroika* proceeds forward from the wreckage made by the Angel's traumatic entry at the end of *Millennium*. A membrane has broken; there is disarray and debris". While the intentional fallacy may problematize any assertion of authorial intention, it is perhaps useful to consider what Kushner himself considers the procession and development from the wreckage to be. In the scattered, delightfully haphazard (perhaps unconsciously reflecting the complex kaleidoscope of the play itself) various notes, acknowledgments and general ruminations which appear before and after the text of *AA2* Kushner offers insightful, if perhaps mystifyingly contradictory ruminations on the play. At the most basic level he argues that *AA1* and *AA2* are "very different plays" but then includes the following quote from Emerson,

> Because the soul is progressive,
> it never quite repeats itself,
> but in every act attempts the production
> of a new and fairer whole.

This almost apologetic note warrants a whole page of its own, and seems to pre-empt those critics who have suggested that *AA2* is merely an opportunistic rehashing of *AA1*, almost along the lines of the purely commercial motivations behind Hollywood sequels.[1] We will discuss Chaos in more detail later, but the apparent contradiction in Kushner's thinking suggests the complexity of fractal science/art in which the same object or formula is constantly different and yet constantly the same. The same characters, themes and dramaturgical devices are used in the plays, but Kushner insists that the plays are "very different." This is difficult to explain. A similar difficulty appears in the "Afterword" to the text of *AA2*. Kushner gracefully acknowledges the help of Oskar Eustis who, among other contributions, helped Kushner create "the optimistic heart of the plays" (157), but within less than a page he eloquently states that "the world howls without; it is at the moment a very terrible world" and that "we help each other … amidst the gathering dark" (158). How can one be optimistic about a world in which your people are being systematically destroyed by an apparently invincible disease which the powers-that-be know little about, and seemingly care even less? Perhaps we may see the paradoxes and contradictions in some of Kushner's thoughts as a positive *jouissance* rather than merely fuzzy-headedness. Consider the end of this "Afterword:"

> Marx was right: the smallest divisible human unit is two people, not one; one is a fiction. From such nets of souls societies, the social world, human life springs. And also plays. (158)

Roy, Harper and Prior all seek the joys of "two" while preserving the integrity and respect of one, and also wish to avoid the chaos and destructive confusion of many more than two, in which the individual becomes totally lost. It is a delicate balancing act, and while the world may indeed be "terrible" there is also, wonderfully, time for play. With this realization that truth may be found in contradiction and an odd unity in paradox, let us consider how the characters face this new world.

AA2 commences with a mixture of humour, despair, ironic stasis and fleeting hope. It opens on "the oldest living Bolshevik" who happens to be "unbelievably old and totally blind" (13) Despite his apparently unpromising physical condition, the old man states the major dilemmas faced by the characters:

> The Great Question before us is: Are we Doomed? The
> Great Question before us is: Will the Past release us? The
> Great Question before us is: Can we Change? In Time?
> And we all desire that Change will come.
>   (*Little pause.*)
> (*With sudden, violent passion.*) And *Theory*? How are we to
> produce without theory? (13)

Kushner gives the opening a seemingly political bent:—the leftover
from the old, discredited system of communism muses ominously
on the lack of any new systems. His old "Theory" did not work, and,
of course, neither does capitalism, with its "market incentives ...
American Cheeseburgers" (14). Capitalism has expanded, amoeba-
like, into the vacuum left by communism, but the old man suggests
that it is only a little less discredited than the system which it
replaces. The old systems are *not* solved by simply replacing one
"ism" with another. Here is the truly revolutionary message of
Kushner's "political" theatre: the malaise and anomie of the
postmodern world lie in deeper, more metaphysical soil, they lie in
the premature ending of all systems. We are left in a frightening
situation:

> If a snake shed his skin before a new skin is ready, naked
> he will be in the world, prey to the forces of chaos.
> Without his skin he will be dismantled, lose coherence
> and die. Have you, my little serpents, a new skin? (13)

Well, have we?

All depends on the type of skin one had before the shedding. The
major narrative themes (and skins) of *AA2* are the fates of Prior
Walter and Roy Cohn. Prior, as the reluctant Prophet of the as-of-yet
unexplained Message, and Roy, as the odious prophet (vehicle) for
laissez-faire Reaganism would appear to have little in common. But
they are both full-blown PWAs. The different manners in which they
react to the disease are vital to the quandary of what is left after the
"isms" have disappeared. *AA2* is hardly a simple play, in fact it is
deliciously complicated. Kushner does not set up a Roy Cohn world-
view versus Prior Walter world-view scenario, and thus avoids the
obvious moral and political conclusions that reducing the play to
such a diatribe might produce. There is no Absolute Right or Wrong.
There are merely—profoundly—shades of grey. Roy is far from the

one-dimensional reptile that he might be: Kushner adds fascinating nuances of near gentleness to him. And the last image, as we shall see, is wonderfully ambiguous. Prior is also complex, as his some-what unexpected reaction to the Angel epitomizes:

> ALESKII: Then we dare not, we cannot, we MUST not move ahead!
> ANGEL: Greetings Prophet!
> The Great Work Begins:
> The Messenger has arrived.
> PRIOR: Go away. (15)

The Red Flag of Communism is flown out, replaced by the Angel with her still mysterious message ... but all Prior has to say is "go away." The bitter representative of the old (Aleskii) and the unwill-ing representative of the new (Prior) are both mired in a spiritual, ethical, philosophical and physical stasis. But while Prior can dis-miss what the Angel has to *say* he cannot reject what she does, or rather, what he does in her presence. She has a wonderfully unex-pected effect upon him: she gives him his "first goddam orgasm in months" (22) and even while he "slept through it," it at least gives him the urge to communicate with other people again. Prior phones Belize, confiding that he is feeling "lascivious, sad ... wonderful and horrible all at once ... and also full of ... joy or something" (23–24). The Angel's presence and message were negatively ambiguous in *AA1*, in *AA2* the ambiguity is transformed into a clear (if initially tentative) message of hope. There is uncertainty to Prior's paradoxi-cal, conflicting emotions and the Angel's message is still unclear, but at least she provokes the solidly positive reaction of an orgasm.

While the first view of Roy in *AA2* is solidly negative, a similar, tentative hope of better things to come gradually develops. But his initial reaction upon seeing Belize is to demand "a white nurse ... my constitutional right" (26) and then continues with the charming command for Belize not to "start jabbing that goddamned spigot in my arm till you find the fucking vein" with the threat to "sue you so bad they'll repossess your teeth you dim black motherf ..." (26). Belize takes this abuse quietly for a while, but he soon counters with a threat which calms Roy in a second:

> BELIZE: Now I've been doing drips a long time. I can slip this in so easy you'll think you were born with it. Or I

      can make it feel like I hooked up a bag of Liquid Drano.
      So you be nice to me or you're going to be one sorry
      asshole come morning.
ROY: Nice.
BELIZE: Nice and quiet.
      (*He puts the drip needle in Roy's arm.*)
      There.
ROY: (*Fierce.*) I hurt. (27)

Power is subtly but definitely transferred from Roy to Belize; despite
the subsequent meanderings of their relationship, Roy never entirely
has the upper hand again. It is the first time we have seen him utterly
vulnerable—a vulnerability based, not on the weakness of his
amorality or the odiousness of his politics, but upon the simple,
physical vulnerability his AIDS-condition places him in. Belize
appreciates that this vulnerability may be used to reveal a different
side to Roy, it allows him to (perhaps unwillingly) prove that there
is more to him than the one-dimensional racist attacks. Later in the
scene Roy asks Belize to "sit … talk" (28), provoking a, perhaps
parodic, stream of invective from the nurse:

    BELIZE: Mr. Cohn, I'd rather suck the pus out of an
      abscess. I'd rather drink a subway toilet. I'd rather chew
      my tongue off and spit it in your leathery face. So
      thanks for the offer of conversation, but I'd rather not.
      (*Belize starts to exit, turning off the light as he does.*)
    ROY: Oh forchristsake. What I gotta do? Beg? I don't want
      to be alone.
    (*Belize stops.*) (28)

Why does Belize stop? Having previously gained control, Belize now
shows what he will do with it. Faced with the death of a man he has
every reason to loathe he simply "*stops,*" and in that stopping there
is communication, empathy, even compassion. Belize also advises
Roy not to get the treatment his doctor is suggesting, telling him of
the AZT tests which are just commencing. Ironically, Belize is helping a man he despises towards the possibility of at least a little more
life. But, like the strangely ambivalent joy that Prior feels with the
Angel, neither Roy nor Belize understand quite why he is being so
helpful:

ROY: You hate me.
BELIZE: Yes.
ROY: Why are you telling me this?
BELIZE: I wish I knew. (30)

With both Roy and Prior there is a quiet optimism in the midst of their deterioration. True enough, Prior is left disturbed by his mysterious visions and unexpected orgasms, and Roy resorts to blackmail to get his stash of AZT, but each scene has a smiling ambivalence at its heart. The closeted gay right-winger who willingly compares himself to "public lice" and the overtly gay, black male nurse—this might be an irreconcilably confrontational situation, yet they gain a form of understanding. The dying AIDS patient visited by a female Angel who speaks in rather ungrammatical, mysterious platitudes—yet the PWA experiences the first orgasm he has had in months. Paradoxes, true, but these are paradoxes foretelling a brighter future. The catalyst for this brightness, this potential optimism, is AIDS. While murderously destructive, the disease is starting to strip away the pretensions, conceits and fears inherent to Prior and Roy. It is enabling, or forcing them to face the reality of their selves without these protections.

As Roy and Prior find the routes of escape closed, so in act two, scene 2 the Angel finally reveals herself and her message. Previously she has just been a highly impressive, if fleeting, presence hovering on the edges of *AA1* and *AA2*. But in this scene she not only arrives … she stays. But this is no Conversion on the Road to Damascus: neither Prophet nor Angel seems entirely sure of what is happening. Prior believes that he is going blind ("my eyes are fucked up" [42]), but also that he is some kind of "prophet" (43), and then the meeting with the Angel is shown in its entirety. This is the *third* time that the Angel's entry has been seen—encapsulating both the delay, fragmentation and importance of her vision. But she is hardly the omniscient/omnipotent Angel of popular tradition, rather one confused by incomplete and perhaps contradictory facts. She speaks with an oddly clumsy type of verbosity of "the True Great Vocalist, the Knowing Mind, Tongue-of-the-Land, Seer-Head" (44), and then tells Prior to "Remove from their hiding place the Sacred Prophetic Implements" (44), only to discover that he has never heard of them. The Angel thinks that Prior's "dreams have revealed them" (45), but Prior simply states that "I haven't had a dream I can remember in months" (45). The confusion provokes a vitally important response from the Angel:

> ANGEL: Quiet. Prophet. A moment, please, I … The
> disorganization is … (*She coughs, looks up*). He says he
> hasn't had any …
> (*Coughs.*)
> Yes.
> In the kitchen. Under the tiles under the sink. (45)

The Angel moves from the fluid verbal diarrhea of her previous messages to a fragmented confusion, during which she coughs. The cough will assume much larger significance a little later in my argument, but on its first appearance it gives an oddly human quality of physical imperfection/vulnerability to the Angel. Prior goes to the kitchen to recover the Sacred Implements following a "revision in the text" (46), and discovers that the Implements are in fact a large book and a pair of bronze binoculars. Prior puts the binoculars on but then thrusts them away, saying, "that was terrible … I don't want to see *that*" (46). What Prior actually sees through the apparently solid binoculars is never revealed, so even in this scene of "revelation" some aspects are kept from the audience, much as the full picture apparently eludes Prior and the Angel.

The uncertainty as to the actual order of events in the Revelation is soon replaced by the certainties of the Angel's physical effects on Prior. They indulge in a bizarre form of verbal sex in which Prior starts to "*hump the book*" while the Angel chants in his ear such memorable nothings as "the Universe Aflame with Angelic Ejaculate" and "the Heavens A-thrum to the Seraphic Rut" (48). While Prior and the Angel experience simultaneous orgasm the sex is merely a brief respite from the uncertainties and confusion of their position. Their sex is bizarre, but at least it is total and self-absorbing while it lasts. Sex leads into more uncertainty as Prior reveals that the Angels "used to copulate *ceaselessly* before …"(49), but he cannot say before what. The truth is too painful and so he describes how they are "basically incredibly powerful bureaucrats," but they have "no imagination" (49). It is this *imagination* which has made humanity so dangerous and ultimately destructive:

ANGEL: In creating You, Our Father-Lover unleashed
   Sleeping Creation's Potential for Change. In You the
   Virus of TIME began. (49)

Here is the central dilemma: humanity has imagination and the
ability to change events. This "change" is not merely the shuffling of
pre-existing conditions (the type of change catalysed by the Angels)
but a far more powerful form, a power to change completely, irrevocably. A power to transform, but also a power to destroy. Mankind
is thus a kind of AIDS of the universe, or perhaps more precisely, it
is the HIV of the Universe—an apparently insignificant entity which
breaks old conditions, dissolves the status-quo (immune system) of
the universe, allowing Chaos (AIDS) to ensue. God does not battle
Man over this but merely absconds, on the day of the 1906 San
Francisco Earthquake! The old positions are reversed:

ANGEL: Paradise itself Shivers and Splits, Each day when
   You awake, as though WE are only the Dream of YOU.
   PROGRESS! MOVEMENT! (50)

And then, in the midst of the Angel's description of the Destruction
of the Universe ... Belize interrupts:

ANGEL: ... Made drear and barren, missing Him.
   (*She coughs*)
BELIZE: Abandoned.
PRIOR: Yes.
BELIZE: I smell a motif. The man that got away. (55)

Kushner constantly undercuts the most powerful, apparently
"dramatic" moments, much as the "*cough*" signals doom for the
Angel. The Angel is infected with the HIV of the universe: Man.
However much she may terrify and eloquently persuade, she is
always infected. She echoes Prior's and Roy's apparently futile strug-
gling against their own AIDS. Like the strange similarity/dissonance
of Chaos science and the fractal view of the world thus produced,
human AIDS is part of a larger pattern, a pattern of eternal invasion,
destruction and eventual self-destruction. Consider Arnold
Schnitzler's comments from a period decades before the appearance
of AIDS:

This human being, whom we think of as afflicted by
disease, is the microbe's landscape, its world. And for

these minuscule individuals, to strive unconsciously and involuntarily to destroy this world of theirs, and to often succeed in so doing, is the basic requirement and the entire meaning of their existence ... might it not then be surmised that from the standpoint of some higher organism, humanity itself is a sickness; that the existence of humanity has this organism as prerequisite, as basic requirement, as meaning, and that we are forever striving—indeed, obliged —to destroy it progressively as we develop just as the microbes strive to destroy the human individual "afflicted by disease"? (Quoted in Baudrillard, 1993, 161)

All are linked through viral transmission, a viral network of infinitely changing yet constantly similar interlinkage. The viral system of which AIDS is just a part is the infinite line contained within the finite space. It is the Strange Attractor of Chaos theory. All is movement, and yet all is trapped. The Angel says that "STASIS" is the only cure for the universe's ills ... and Man's perhaps. But it is the apparent stasis of modern man's psyche which catalyses the endless search for truth, for an escape from the conclusions engendered by standing still too long. The ultimate expression of this Age of Anomie is Beckett's "*they do not move*," but the Angel pleads with Prior to persuade Man to do precisely this; to do precisely nothing. The "NEW LAW" is paradoxical, contradictory and perhaps destructive. Humanity is defined by Imagination and Movement, as the Angel herself eloquently expresses, but at the same time it must "Seek Not to Fathom the World and its Delicate Particle Logic" (52). To save the universe (and itself?), Humanity must desist from those activities which define it. The Angel ignores the inevitable illogicality of all viruses, whether they be human or otherwise: they are destined by their very nature to destroy the environment which supports them, and thus to destroy themselves. Humanity, unlike the Angels, has the power of Imagination—it possesses the God-like ability to create something out of nothing. Indeed, the very "Particle Logic" which the Angel mentions involves the intricacies of sub-atomic physics in which particles spontaneously appear and disappear without any apparent causative agent. If humanity discovers the secrets of these processes then God will truly merely become the Dream of Man, for God will no longer have the strength, or the will, to battle his creation. Human AIDS may be the last-ditch effort of God. If it fails, Man will either become God … or at least supplant him. If God is Frankenstein and Man is the Creature, then the Creature not only kills his Creator, he also becomes the Creator and learns in turn how to produce something out of nothing. More importantly, Man's viral nature will lead to the opposite tendency— the constant movement and growth will lead us to destroy everything; to create nothing from something.

Prior is the viral agent introduced into Man as Organism, designed to intervene in the process outlined above. The rest of the play evaluates how successful or otherwise the Angel is in planting the Message (Virus) in this manner. Prior sets himself on the line of prophets which stretches from Tiresias through John and onwards, but unlike them he is still ready to "run"—to escape the implications of his duties as prophet. He is a reluctant prophet, forced into a stasis through his disease, but hardly ready for the permanent stasis which the Angel requires. Strangely, Prior is hardly the ideal candidate for a prophet in the traditional sense: his lover has left him, he has hardly any friends, he is indeed a "sick, lonely man" (53)—who is he to bring his message and new law to? The answer comes from Prior himself, as he suggests that the message may lie not in words but in his very existence, maybe the most powerful effect comes with the image of "all of us who are dying now" (55). This is, of course, vitally different from the Angel's position—she wants a specific message, a specific effect—stasis. But for Prior *all* those with AIDS are part of an overall prophecy, whatever their particular "message" might be.

Act three opens on that other prophet, Roy, in a rapidly deteriorating situation as "… *the pain in his gut is constant and getting worse*" (57). He now also possesses "*a more elaborate phone system*" than before, but one which only serves to connect him with devilish precision to the unpleasant facts of the past: i.e., he is being investigated by a Senate Committee for corruption. Neither Roy nor Prior is prepared to sit still, even though they both have ample reason/ excuse to do so because they are dying of AIDS. Neither PWA is ready to take stock of the past—they each cling to the hope of a future. Each is inevitably, irrevocably part of the eternal commutability of the postmodern sign. Signified leads to signified, image to image, unfounded hope to unfounded hope—the world has forgotten about the logical need for concrete, stable, easily identifiable signifieds. The Angel seeks a return to the simple Saussaurean system of the static duality of signifier/ied, but Roy with his desperate need to maintain contact, to preserve his place on the Baudrillardian "smooth surface of communication" exemplifies the futility of the Angel's wishes.

They can move, but Roy and Prior are rapidly losing pragmatic power—Roy seeks to keep his stash of AZT to himself, but Belize and the ghost of Ethel Rosenberg are too much for him. Roy's insults are merely futile screams into a howling gale. Belize takes the pills and Ethel decides to visit his disbarment proceedings. Roy understands his position too late to do anything about it, at least in this life:

> ROY: Fucking SUCCUBUS! Fucking bloodsucking old bat!
> (He picks up the phone, punches a few buttons and then puts the receiver back, dejectedly.)
> The worst thing about being sick in America, Ethel, is you are booted out of the parade. Americans have no use for the sick. (62)

Prior, who never had a central role in practical American society, finds it easier to fulfill the role of outcast. When he meets Harper in the bizarre Mormon Diorama he tells her that he is "doing research" as he is now an "Angelologist"; the Angel's bizarre appearance and message have led the prophet to do precisely the opposite of what the divine being wanted, as Prior states that "I should be in bed but I'm too anxious to lie in bed" (64). He is trying to assign some kind of meaning to his recent experiences, a frame of reference. Prior is using his imagination, he is curious, he seeks to progress beyond the dazed confusion which apparently afflicts him ... he is doing everything the Angel opposes. Both Prior and Harper seek enlightenment through imaginative reconstruction, but the Mormon Diorama doesn't work properly, the voice tape plays either too slow or too fast, and the movement of the dummies is stilted— "the father's face moves, but not his body" (65). Confusion and wisdom embrace as Harper seems bizarrely privy to the Angel's message and strange vernacular:

> PRIOR: Imagination is a dangerous thing.
> HARPER: (Looking at the face of the dummy.) In certain circumstances, fatal. It can blow up in your face. If it turns out to be true, threshold ...

PRIOR AND HARPER: ... of revelation.
(*They look at each other.*) (70–71)

Prior has already passed the "threshold" of revelation, but he seems none-the-wiser as a result. Harper knows the words, but not the meaning; she gloomily reminisces about nineteenth-century America, but is soon interrupted by Prior:

Come on.
(*They exit.*) (72)

The "*exit*" is perhaps the best actual representation of "the new law" for this Age of Anomie. The Beckettian stasis which the Angels seek is untenable, for both Prior and Harper find life terribly ambivalent and unstructured. Each is compelled to constantly move, much as Roy vainly tries to preserve his previous powers of remote communication. These postmodern nihilists are compelled by their Sysyphean task of being caught in an untenable present, between nostalgia for a past which probably never existed and an utterly uncertain future. The tentatively promising future for Prior early in *AA2* is transformed into a ceaseless physical, spiritual and mental wandering, and wondering.

Roy's next scene is highly optimistic in comparison. He is lost in a morphine haze, but one which has apparently brought out his kinder, gentler nature. He becomes hilariously sexual and sensual with the nurse whom, in his more "lucid" moments, he despises. Roy wants Belize's "dark strong arms" to, as he says, "squeeze the bloody life out of me," and ultimately to "just open me up to the end of me" (76). This opening is physical in the most obvious sense but Roy also seeks a kind of spiritual opening, as he asks the nurse to describe heaven for him. Belize obliges, and uncannily describes heaven as being "like San Francisco" (77). While knowledge and the message are hardly concrete entities in *AA2*, their intangibility is compensated for by the breadth of their dissemination. Prior has direct access to the message, characters such as Belize and Harper obtain an intuitive, instinctive understanding of it—but all of them relate it to the City by the Bay. God absconds on the day of the 1906 Earthquake. This is, of course, *before* the great scientific leaps of this century which have led Man to the brink of understanding the "delicate particle logic," bringing him to the edge of fulfilling his role as/in the Virus of Time. God can see into the future—he is omnis-

cient, but, like his Angels, is far from omnipotent. Utter clarity of
vision and total inability to act create an unacceptable agony ... and
so he absconds. While Belize's vision of heaven-without-God is
initially rather dismal, "on every corner a wrecking crew ... windows
missing in every edifice like broken teeth, fierce gusts of gritty wind"
(77), he soon cheers up as the people inhabiting this apparent
wilderness are a living embodiment of the "melting pot" theory once
regarded as gospel, but currently challenged:

> BELIZE: And all the deities are Creole, mulatto, brown as
>   the mouths of rivers.
> (Roy laughs again.)
> BELIZE: Race, taste and history finally overcome. And
>   you ain't there. (77–78)

Chaos, destruction, a permanent construction site, a sulking/absent
God, an endless mixing of race ... and people like Roy aren't there.
A superficially heavenly heaven, perhaps? But history is finished:
humanity has stopped its apparently insatiable hunger for knowledge. Progress has ceased. The tenuousness of this vision can be
gleaned from the method of its delivery and receipt—Belize can only
describe it in the guise of a soft, emotional torture while Roy can
only understand it while lost in morphine. Neither really concedes
to the logical conclusions of the vision. As Roy drifts nearer to death
the communication fragments, Belize becomes merely, as he tells
Roy, "the shadow on your grave" (78). Roy portrays himself as some
inhuman machine, telling Joe that "I'm tough ... its taking a lot ... to
dismantle me" (83). Increasingly avoided by the living (Belize, Joe,
etc.) and shunned by the dead (Ethel), Roy is an isolated figure as he
rambles in a no-man's-land between the living and the dead.

Early in act four, Kushner accentuates the distance between those
with AIDS and those without, between the prophets and their un-
willing followers. In a split scene he places Roy and Prior with their
respective ex-lovers. While Roy and Joe seem to reach some sort of
brief understanding, Prior and Louis remain hopelessly alienated.
Louis has come to explain why he has been so cruel ... not to plead
with Prior to take him back. Prior, faced once again with an unavoidable and yet unbearable situation, falls back on his newly found
position in the universe,

PRIOR: Fuck you. I'm a prophet. (85)

and then the distance between the pairs of lovers is accentuated with the beautiful ironic-commentary that the split-scene device enables:

PRIOR: You cry, but you endanger nothing in yourself.
It's like the idea of crying when you do it. Or the idea
of love.
ROY: Now you have to go.
JOE: I left my wife.
(*Little pause.*)
I needed to tell you.
ROY: It happens. (85)

The two PWAs, desperate to remain part of the "normal" world, illustrate an other-worldly remoteness from it. As Roy sinks into death, Ethel serenades him in his final moments with a cruelly ironic song. The death is ambiguous, powerful, disturbing:

ROY: (*in a very faint voice.*) Next time around I don't want
to be a man. I wanna be an octopus. Remember that,
OK? A fucking ...
(*pushing an imaginary button with his finger.*)
Hold.
(*He dies.*) (115)

Is this all Roy ever was? Was he merely a kind of super mobile telephone, a characterless cipher for vicarious but vicious information? The "hold" may be threatening: Roy may be dead, but what he represents is repeated interminably. Another self-defeating, self-denying bigot will appear to release the hold button and continue the cycle of ill-gotten privilege and destruction. Roy the individual man is dead, but death of the individual is not important in this play. It is the conflict, clash and destruction of ideas that is important—individuals may drift interminably, or return to the earth as ghosts. Ideas, once shattered, are irreparable. Roy's ideas are far from beaten, they are merely, and ominously, put on hold.

Roy is gone, but only temporarily; ghosts are as real, if not more real, in this world than mortal human beings. With the Angel's return Prior seeks to reject his role as prophet, to disown the Angel. Remarkably, we find that the Angel is not merely a product of Prior's imagination, because Hannah sees her too. The nominally religious woman is faced, not with a metaphoric vision easy to laugh at and theorize about, but with a vigorous, physical reality. The wrestling match combines an obvious parody on religious tradition with the seemingly mystical, and throws in physical slapstick for good measure. The Angel and Prior communicate far better through the wrestling and resulting verbal exchange than through much of their previous semantic gymnastics. The Angel complains that "I have torn a muscle in my thigh," thus blaming her loss and Prior's subsequent return to heaven with the book on a pettily trivial injury. The wrestling itself is clumsy, odd, but strangely compelling and bonding. It is much like the sex between the Angel and mortals, a theme which immediately reappears as the Angel kisses Hannah on the lips and instantly gives her "*an enormous orgasm*" (120). The Angel has the last laugh. As a representative of the Divine Order of the Universe her great sexual powers (as opposed to her hilariously illustrated verbal and physical limitations) are vital. Man may be progressing at such an unstoppable rate that even God relinquishes control, but Man is still vulnerable to the sexual. Prior gets uncontrollable erections every time the Angel appears, the Angel can give orgasms to a sexually repressed, middle-aged religious zealot. If sexuality is the driving force behind humanity's endless search for progress (and "Angelic orgasm makes protomatter" [119], making the sexual the dominant creative force in the universe), it is also the force over which humanity has the least control. Each of us runs after our own destruction—the desire for movement, for change is universal, and this is a Janus-faced desire: on one side is the creative drive, on the other the drive to destroy. Prior seems uneasy with both creativity and destruction—lacking the energy for the former and the ruthlessness for the latter. It is Roy who, whatever moral judgment one might want to pass on him, exhibits a potentiality for both.

Roy is dead, but even as Prior ascends to heaven, his presence is still felt. The heavenly meeting is no classical *deus ex machina*, nor is it renaissance enlightenment, nor even a Nietzschean destruction of the divine—this is a coalescing of confused mortal and even more confused supernatural. The walls of heaven are covered with "*much cracked plaster*" (123), and the Angels vainly try to organize the "*heaps and heaps and heaps of books and files and bundles of yellowing newspapers*" (128)—heaven is an odd mixture of Dickensian decay and postmodern chaos. The physical disorganization reflects a mental disarray, but while the initial conversation between Prior and the Angels is confusing, it soon hones in on basic, mutual problems:

> PRIOR: I ... I want to return this.
> *(He holds out the book, no-one takes it from him.)*
> AUSTRALIA: What is the matter with it?
> PRIOR: *(A beat, then)* It's just ... it's just ... We can't just stop. We're not rocks—progress, migration, motion is ... modernity. It's *animate*, it's what living things do. We desire. Even if all we desire is stillness, it's still desire *for* ... (132)

The Angels, immortal but desireless, stare at the man who is mortal and yet desireful. The void between them is immense, seemingly uncrossable. But they are linked by a common suffering, as eventually the Plague of Man and the Plague of the Universe are considered, with equally gloomy prognoses:

> PRIOR: I haven't *done* anything yet, I ... I want to be healthy again. And this plague, it should stop. In me and everywhere. Make it go away.
> AUSTRALIA: Oh We have tried.
> We suffer with You but
> We do not know. We
> Do not know how.
> *(Prior and Australia look at each other.)* (134)

The "*look*" contains the agony of their isolation and the empathy of their shared experience. Prior leaves heaven with the repeated refrain that "I want more life." It is a simple desire, one the Angels are powerless to deny but equally powerless to grant. Prior seeks "more life," but he is caught within the rather narrow definition of life as the endless movement towards ... and endless desire for ... he knows not what. Roy, although he has lost his own battle for mortal existence, is doing remarkably well for himself in the hereafter. The bricoleur, improvisational tactics of the sinuously amoral, recently deceased Cohn bring him a star client:

> *As Prior journeys to earth he sees Roy, at a great distance, in Heaven, or Hell, or Purgatory—standing waist-deep in a smoldering pit, facing a volcanic, pulsating red light ...*

> ROY: Paternity suit? Abandonment? Family court is my
> particular matter, I'm an absolute fucking demon with
> Family law ... Yes, I will represent you, King of the
> Universe, yes I will sing and eviscerate ... (139)

Prior is the Chosen one, the Prophet selected from all of humanity to deliver the Angel's Message, but it is Roy who slips off the mortal coil so easily, and it is Roy who slides so easily into his new role as God's lawyer. Disbarred on earth, he becomes the King of the Universe's counsel. More than this, Roy (and all he represents) seems to surpass God, to replace him in the cosmic order of control. It is the type of endless movement and progress represented by Roy that is so insidious and powerful, it is he that cannot be stopped. While the final, nominally optimistic message of the play is left to Prior, Kushner leaves Roy with the power. The final speech is an uneasy mixture of pep-talk, political diatribe and ironic contemplation:

> This disease will be the end of many of us, but not
> nearly all, and the dead will be commemorated and will
> struggle on with the living, and we are not going away.
> We won't die secret deaths anymore. The world only spins
> forward. We will be citizens. The time has come.
> Bye now.
> You are fabulous creatures, each and every one.
> And I bless you: *More Life*.
> The Great Work begins. (148)

While this ending may be the crystallization of the "optimistic heart" which Kushner identifies in his plays (a suggestion I find problematic at best), I feel that Declan Donellan's interpretation of this speech in the National Theatre production best exemplifies the rich ambivalence and ambiguity which provides much of the fascination and impact of both plays. Donellan staged the speech, not as some triumphant avowal of hope, but as a tentative improvisation of vitality in a both literally and metaphorically gathering darkness. The stage lights slowly faded to black as Prior delivered the final sentences with steadily diminishing volume. The final, "great work begins" was a whisper, almost inaudible to me even though I was seated on the front row just a couple of feet from Prior. The "life" which Prior clings to with such tenacity is merely a faint glimmer in the rapidly encroaching doom. Prior may be alive at the end of *AA2*, and thus victorious in the most basic sense, but it is a Pyrrhic victory. He still speaks of "the world spinning forward" and of "fabulous creatures"—clearly the Angel's mission to infect Man with Viral Stasis has failed. The Angel fails, Prior fails (he is still inexorably dying by degrees) and God fails.

Only Roy Cohn is triumphant.

AIDS is not a Saviour for Reality in the face of Hyper-reality; in fact, the diametric opposite is true—it catalyses, crystallizes and eventually embodies the simulacrous heart of the hyper-real. The final message is one of despair, the Great Work is merely a repetitive cycle of anomie.

The PWA encapsulates humanity's fate ...

Notes

1. In a conversation with the author, Mel Gordon (Professor of Theatre at U.C. Berkeley) suggested that we might see *Angels in America* Parts 3, 4, 5 ... like the *Nightmare on Elm Street* series.

Works Cited

Baudrillard, Jean. "The Ecstasy of Communication." *The Anti-Aesthetic: Essays on Postmodern Culture*. Ed. Hal Foster. Seattle: Bay Press, 1983.

————. *The Transparency of Evil*. London: Verso, 1993.

Emerson, Ralph Waldo. "On Art." *Collected Works*. Ed. N. Spiller. Harvard University Press, 1971.

Husserl, Edmund. *Logical Investigations*. Halle, 1900.

Kushner, Tony. *Angels in America, Part One: Millenium Approaches*. New York: Theatre Communications Group, 1994.

Kushner, Tony. *Angels in America, Part Two: Perestroika*. New York: Theatre Communications Group, 1994.

Nietzsche, Fredrich. "The Dawn." *Portable Nietzsche*. Penguin, 1964.

Osborn, Elizabeth M. *The Way We Live Now: American Plays and the AIDS Crisis*. New York: Theatre Communicatons Group, 1990.

Pinter, Harold. "Between the Lines." *The Sunday Times* (4 March 1962): 39.

Rich, Frank. "Angels' angels;" *New York Times*. (25 April 1993): 29.

Springsteen, Bruce. "The Streets of Philadelphia." Song from the movie *Philadelphia*. Tristar Pictures, 1993.

States, Bert. *Great Reckonings in Little Rooms: On the Phenomenology of Theatre*. Berkeley: UC Press, 1985.

Acknowledgements

I wish to acknowledge the editorial, intellectual and spiritual input of Amy Glynn to this piece. It wouldn't exist without her.

The Theatre of the Fabulous

Interview by David Savran

Nicki van Templehoff and Zazie de Paris
in *Engle in America*. Photo © Matthias Horn.

The Theatre of the Fabulous:
An Interview with Tony Kushner

by David Savran

When Bill Kushner diligently guided his 14-year-old son Tony through Wagner's 20-hour *Ring* cycle, he little suspected his prodigious offspring would end up some two decades later writing *the* theatrical epic of the 1990s.

Angels in America, with its ground-breaking Broadway run scheduled to continue through January '95, has now begun a national tour in Chicago while theatres around the world scramble to mount their own productions of the play. From A.C.T. in San Francisco to the Alley in Houston, from the Intiman in Seattle to the Alliance in Atlanta, theatres across America are scheduling the seven-hour, two-part play as the centrepiece of their 1994–95 seasons. At the same time, audiences in seventeen foreign countries (including France, Germany, Japan, Iceland and Brazil) will have an opportunity over the next year to see productions of the most widely acclaimed and produced new American play in memory.

From its inception—commissioned by San Francisco's Eureka Theatre Company, it was mounted in workshop and full productions at the Eureka, Los Angeles's Mark Taper Forum and London's Royal National Theatre prior to its April 1993 opening on Broadway— *Angels in America: A Gay Fantasia on National Themes* has changed

---

DAVID SAVRAN's most recent book is *Communists, Cowboys, and Queers: The Politics of Masculinity in the Work of Arthur Miller and Tennessee Williams*. He is professor of English at Brown University. An abridged version of this interview appeared in *American Theater*, October, 1994.

the face and scale of the American theatre. Having amassed the Pulitzer Prize for Drama, two best-play Tonys, and a spate of other prestigious awards, it has proven, against all odds, that a play can tackle the most controversial and difficult subjects—politics, sex, disease, death and religion—and still find a large and diverse audience. This achievement is even more remarkable when one considers that all five of its leading male characters are gay. Bringing together Jews and Mormons, African- and European-Americans, neo-conservatives and leftists, closeted gay men and exemplars of the new "queer politics," *Angels* is indeed a gay fantasia, writing a history of America in the age of Reagan and the age of AIDS.

Tony Kushner, a self-described "red-diaper baby," was raised in Lake Charles, Louisiana, the son of professional musicians. The Kushner's rambling house on the edge of a swamp teemed with pets and resounded with music. Young Tony developed an appreciation of opera and the Wagnerian scale of events from his father (*Moby Dick* remains Tony's favourite novel), while from his mother, Sylvia's involvement in amateur theatrics, he learned to appreciate the emotional power of theatre. (He still vividly remembers her performance as Linda Loman in *Death of a Salesman*—and the tremendous identification he felt with her.) But at age six, when he developed a crush on Jerry, his Hebrew school teacher, he knew he was not like the other boys. Growing up, as he puts it, "very, very closeted," he was intrigued by the sense of disguise theatre could offer. And because he had decided "at a very early age" that he would *become* heterosexual, he avoided the theatre in town, where he knew he would find other gay men.

In the mid-1970s, he moved to New York to attend Columbia, where he studied medieval art, literature and philosophy, and read the works of Karl Marx for the first time. Still fascinated with theatre, however, he explored the ground-breaking experimental work of directors like Richard Foreman, Elizabeth LeCompte, JoAnne Akalaitis and Charles Ludlam, immersed himself in the classical and modernist theatre traditions, and got involved in radical student politics. It was not until after he graduated from Columbia, however, that he began to come out. And much like Joe Pitt in *Millennium Approaches*, he called his mother from a pay phone in the East Village to tell her he was gay.

Angels in America pays energetic tribute to these diverse experiences and inspirations. Drawing on Brecht's political theatre, on the innovations of the theatrical avant-garde, and on the solidly American narrative tradition that stretches back to Eugene O'Neill and Tennessee Williams, it invents a kind of camp epic theatre—or in Kushner's phrase, a Theatre of the Fabulous. Spanning the earth and reaching into the heavens, interweaving multiple plots, mixing metaphysics and drag, fictional and historical characters, revengeful ghosts and Reagan's smarmy henchmen, *Angels* demonstrates that reality and fantasy are far more difficult to distinguish than one might think. It also verifies, as political activists have insisted since the 1960s, that the personal is indeed the political: Exploring the sometimes tortuous connections between a personal identity (sexual, racial, religious or gender) and a political position, it dramatizes the seeming impossibility of maintaining one's private good in a world scourged by public greed, disease and hatred.

Yet *Angels in America* is by no means a play about defeat. On the contrary, it consistently attests to the possibility not only of progress but also of radical—almost unimaginable—transfiguration. Its title and preoccupation with this utopian potential, inscribed in even the most appalling moments of history, are derived from an extraordinary mediator—the German-Jewish Marxist philosopher Walter Benjamin. In Benjamin's attempt to sketch out a theory of history in "Theses on the Philosophy of History," written in 1940 as he was attempting to flee the Nazis, this most melancholy of Marxists uses Paul Klee's painting, *Angelus Novus*, to envision an allegory of progress in which the angel of history, his wings outspread, is poised between past and future. Caught between the history of the world, which keeps piling wreckage at his feet, and a storm blowing from Paradise, the angel "would like to stay, awaken the dead, and make whole what has been smashed." But the storm "has got caught in his wings" and propels him blindly and irresistibly into an unknown future.

For Kushner, the angel of history serves as a constant reminder both of catastrophe (AIDS, racism, misogyny and homophobia, to name only the most obvious) and of the perpetual possibility of change, the expectation that, as Benjamin puts it, the tragic continuum of history will be blasted open. And the concept of utopia to which he is linked ensures that the vehicle of enlightenment and hope in *Angels*—the prophet who announces the new age—will be the character who must endure the most pain: Prior Walter, a man born too soon and too late, suffering AIDS and the desertion of his lover. Moreover, in Kushner's reinterpretation of American history, this utopia is inextricably linked both to the extraordinary idealism that has long driven American politics and to the ever-deepening structural inequalities that continue to betray and mock that idealism.

It is hardly coincidental that *Angels in America* should capture the imagination of theatre-goers at this decisive moment in history, at the end of the Cold War, as the United States is attempting to renegotiate its role as the number-one player in the imperialist sweepstakes. More brazenly than any other recent play, *Angels*—not unlike Wagner's *Ring*—takes on questions of national mission and identity. It also attempts to interrogate the various mythologies—from Mormonism to multiculturalism to neoconservatism—that have been fashioned to consolidate an American identity.

At the same time, the play is intent on emphasizing the crucial importance of the sexual and racial margins in defining this elusive identity. In this sense, it seems linked historically to the strategies of a new activist movement, Queer Nation, whose founding in 1990 only narrowly postdates the writing of the play. This offshoot of the AIDS activist group ACT UP agitates for a broader and more radical social and cultural agenda. Like Queer Nation, *Angels in America* aims to subvert the distinction between the personal and the political, to refuse to be closeted, to undermine the category of the "normal," and to question the fixedness and stability of every sexual identity. Reimagining America, giving it a camp inflection, *Angels* announces: "We're here. We're queer. We're fabulous. Get used to it!"

I interviewed Tony Kushner on a cold Sunday afternoon in January 1994 in his Upper West Side apartment.

David Savran: How did you first get interested in theatre?

Tony Kushner: My mother was a professional bassoonist but when we moved down to Louisiana, she didn't have enough playing opportunities so she channelled her creative energies into being an amateur actress. She was the local tragedienne and played Linda Loman and Anne Frank's mother. She also played Anna O in *A Far Country*, her first play, and I had vivid homoerotic dreams about her being carried around by this hot young man who played Sigmund Freud—you can make all sorts of things about that!—and I have very strong memories of her power and the effect she had on people.

I remember her very much in *Death of a Salesman*, everybody weeping at the end of the play. She was really very, very good in those parts. So I think it had something to do with being a mother-defined gay man [laughs] and an identification with her participation.

And then there were other obvious things. I grew up very, very closeted and I'm sure that the disguise of theatre, the doubleness, and all that slightly tawdry stuff, interested me. I acted a little bit when I was a kid but because most of the people who hung around the theatre in town were gay men, I was afraid of getting caught up in that. I had decided at a very early age that I would become heterosexual. So I became a debater instead. And then when I got to New York, I started seeing every play.

DS: When was that?

TK: 1974. I arrived at a pretty great time. Broadway had not died completely. So you could still see some interesting Broadway-type shows: *The Royal Family, Absurd Person Singular*, things that were sort of trashy but really well-done, with actors like Rosemary Harris and Larry Blyden. Musicals were already dead, but there was something that resembled excitement: *Equus, Amadeus*, and all that shit, which I knew wasn't good but at least had energy. And at the same time there was all this stuff going on downtown. I saw the last two performances of Richard Schechner's *Mother Courage* and then I watched as the Performance Group disintegrated and became the Wooster Group. I saw Spalding Gray's first performance pieces and *Three Places in Rhode Island*, Lee Breuer's *Animations* and JoAnne Akalaitis's *Dressed Like an Egg*. And I saw one piece by Foreman, I think it was *Rhoda in Potatoland*, but I didn't understand it. It was the first piece of experimental theatre I'd ever seen and I was horrified and fascinated. My first real experience with Foreman was his *Threepenny Opera* which I saw about 95 times and is one of my great theatre experiences.

When I was in college, I was beginning to read Marx. As a freshman, I had read Ernest Fisher's *The Necessity of Art* and was very upset and freaked out by it. The notion of the social responsibility of artists was very exciting and upsetting for me.

DS: Why upsetting?

TK: I arrived from Louisiana with fairly standard liberal politics. I was ardently Zionist and where I grew up, the enemy was still classic American anti-Semitism. It was a big shock to discover all these people on the left at Columbia who were critical of Israel. My father is very intelligent in politics but very much a child of the Krushchev era, the great disillusionment with Stalinism. I guess I just believed that Marxism was essentially totalitarianism and I could hear in Fisher, and then in Arnold Hauser, a notion of responsibility that is antithetical to the individualist ideology that I hadn't yet started to question.

And there were two things that changed my understanding of theatre. One was reading Brecht. I saw *Threepenny Opera* in '76 and thought it was the most exciting theatre I'd ever seen. It seemed to me to combine the extraordinary visual sense that I had seen downtown with a narrative theatre tradition that I felt more comfortable with. And there was also the amazing experience of the performance. When Brecht is done well, it is both a sensual delight and extremely unpleasant. And Foreman got that as almost nothing I've ever seen. It was excoriating and you left singing the songs. So I read the "Short Organum" and *Mother Courage*—which I still think is the greatest play ever written—and began to get a sense of a politically engaged theatre. When I first came to Columbia I was very involved in trying to get amnesty for draft evaders, and I did a library sit-in in '75, which was a big experience for me. It was the first successful political action I'd ever been involved in. And I met all these people from the Weather Underground who were still hanging out in Morningside Heights and got very deeply into the mythology of radical politics. And in Brecht I think I understood Marx for the first time. I understood materialism, the idea of the impact of the means of production, which in Brecht is an issue of theatrical production. I started to understand the way that labour is disappeared into the commodity form, the black magic of capitalism: the real forces operating in the world, the forces of the economy and commodity production are underneath the apparent order of things.

Because of Brecht I started to think of a career in the theatre. It seemed the kind of thing one could do and still retain some dignity as a person engaged in society. I didn't think that you could just be a theatre artist. That's when I first read Benjamin's *Understanding Brecht* and decided I wanted to do theatre. Before that I was going to become a Medieval Studies professor.

DS: Why?

TK: I loved the Middle Ages and I think there's something very appealing about its art, literature and architecture, but I was slowly getting convinced that it was of no relevance to anything.

DS: What about the Middle Ages? The connection between art and religion?

TK: I have a fantastical, spiritual side. And when I got to Columbia, I was very impressionable. The first class I took was a course in expository writing taught by a graduate assistant who was getting her Ph.D. in Anglo-Saxon literature. So we did *Beowulf*. I found the magic and the darkness of it very appealing and I was very, very moved by—and I still am—being able to read something nine hundred years old, or two thousand years old in the case of the Greeks, and to realize that it isn't in any way primitive. And you also realize—although I don't believe in universal human truths—that there are certain human concerns that go as far back as Euripides or Aeschylus.

DS: And of course Medieval art and culture predates the development of bourgeois individualism ...

TK: Exactly.

DS: Which you go to great pains to critique.

TK: And it's extraordinary to see that great richness can come from societies that aren't individuated in that way. The anonymity of the art is terrifying to a modern person. It's not until very late, really until the beginning of the Renaissance, that you start to have artists identifying themselves. You realize these human beings had a profoundly different sense of the social.

At the same time, I started to get very excited about Shakespeare and Ben Jonson. I directed Jonson's *Bartholomew Fair* as my first production at Columbia, and it was horrible.

DS: It's a very difficult play.

TK: Yes, I know. I didn't start easy—thirty-six parts. I couldn't even find thirty-six actors. One of them didn't speak English and we had to teach him syllabically. And you can't understand most of it anyways because of the references to things that have long since disappeared. But I had fun doing it and decided at that point—although I'd tried writing a couple of things—that I would become a director because I didn't think that I'd ever write anything of significance. I was also attempting to follow in the footsteps of people I really admired like Foreman, Akalaitis and Liz LeCompte. I thought that the best thing to do was to write the text as a director. And so I spent two years answering switchboards at a hotel and two years teaching at a school for gifted children in Louisiana. I directed several things there to get over my fear of directing, *The Tempest*,

Midsummer Night's Dream, and I did my first take at *The Baden-Baden Play For Learning* which I'm beginning to think is, next to *Mother Courage*, the best thing Brecht ever wrote. And then I applied to NYU graduate school in directing because I wanted to work with Carl Weber because he had worked with Brecht—and he looked like Brecht. And at my second attempt—George Wolfe and I just discovered that we were rejected by him in the same year—I got in.

DS: You mention *Bartholomew Fair*, with its multiple plot lines, like your own work, and you also speak of the American narrative tradition with which your writing certainly is engaged.

TK: I think it's completely of that tradition.

DS: What impact have Miller, Williams and O'Neill had on your writing?

TK: Miller, none. I do actually admire *Death of a Salesman*. I think it really is kind of powerful. And I can see how, in its time, it had an immense impact. And it's still hard to watch without sobbing at the end. But some of it is a cheat. It's melodramatic and it has that awful, '50s kind of Herman Wouk-ish sexual morality that's disgusting and irritating. And unfortunately, Miller went around talking about what a tragedy it is, the little man and all that. But it really isn't, it's incredibly pathetic, or bathetic.

I sneered at O'Neill for a long time but I'm beginning to realize that two or three of his plays—not just *Long Day's Journey Into Night*—are amazing. I went back and reread *Long Day's Journey* and found it so complicated and theatrical—it's about theatre in ways that the tradition doesn't allow for.

I've always loved Williams. The first time I read *Streetcar*, I was annihilated. I read as much Williams as I could get my hands on until the late plays started getting embarrassingly bad, although there are some that are much more interesting than I realized. But I loved *Night of the Iguana*. And I've always thought *Orpheus Descending* is a fascinating play, much more fascinating than the Broadway production directed by that Tory weasel, Peter Hall, which I thought was just awful. I'm really influenced by Williams but I'm awestruck by O'Neill. I don't feel that he's much of an influence because he's from a very different tradition with a very different sensibility.

DS: On the other hand, I'm always struck by the utopian longings in *Long Day's Journey*, Edmund's dreams of the sea which, I think, tie into your work.

TK: But O'Neill's utopian longings are inseparable from death. He's a Catholic who doesn't believe in redemption, but in death instead. I was so struck by that in *Moon for the Misbegotten*: the only thing that you've got to look forward to is to rest in peace. Josie's wishing Jamie a quiet time in the grave. It's horrendously bleak and very Irish, isn't it? It's also very New England, the fog people. I don't feel that I'm a fog person. I think I'm a lot more sappy than him. Even Williams, eating the unwashed grape, "as blue as my first lover's eyes," that whole vision that Blanche has of dying at sea has more space and possibility and hope than O'Neill.

I've become very influenced by John Guare whom I think is a very important writer. I have to admit to not being nuts about *Six Degrees of Separation*, which I am confused by, but I think *Landscape of the Body*, the Lydie Breeze plays, *House of Blue Leaves* are amazing. Like Williams, he's figured out a way for Americans to do a kind of stage poetry. He's discovered a lyrical voice that doesn't sound horrendously twee and forced and phony. There are astonishingly beautiful things scattered throughout his work.

DS: As I was watching *Perestroika*, I also thought about Robert Wilson.

TK: Hollow grandiosity [laughs].

DS: But the opening tableau, the spectacle, the angel.

TK: I saw *Einstein on the Beach* at the Met in '76 and was maddened and deeply impressed by it. I'm very ambivalent about Wilson. The best I've ever seen him do—the piece I loved the most—was *Hamletmachine*. I was horrified by what I saw of *Civil Wars*. It really seemed like Nuremberg time—done for Reagan's Hitler Olympics. And what he does to history—and I'm not alone in making this criticism. This notion of Ulysses S. Grant and Clytemnestra and owls and Kachina dancers—excuse me, but what is this? What's going on here?

DS: So you see a complete dehistoricization?

TK: Absolutely. And to what end? What are we saying about history? Because these figures are not neutral, they're not decorative. You do see ghosts of ideas floating through but it just feels profoundly aestheticist in the worst, creepiest way, something with fascist potential. Also, the loudest voice is the voice of capital: this cost so much money, and you've spent so much money, and it's so expensive. There's a really unholy synthesis going on of what is supposed to be resistant, critical and marginal, marrying big money

and big corporate support. He's an amazing artist, but it disturbs me.
I've always felt much more drawn to Foreman and early Akalaitis.
JoAnne did some very interesting things with *Dead End Kids*. And
with Foreman, even if you're completely awash in some
phenomenological sea, you absolutely believe there's a stern, terrifying moral centre, and so much blood and heart in it. What I like
about Wilson, and I felt this watching *Hamletmachine*, is: this is such
tough theatre, this is hard work. I was always afraid of making the
audience work.

DS: Your work does bring together so many of these things:
Brecht, the American narrative tradition, downtown theatre, Caryl
Churchill ....

TK: I left out Maria Irene Fornes. She's very, very important to
me. I got to watch her go from really experimental stuff like *The
Diary of Evelyn Brown*, a pioneer woman who lived on the plains and
made endless, tedious lists of what she did during the day. And
Fornes just staged them. It was monumentally boring and extraordinary. Every once in a while, this pioneer woman would do a little
clog dance. You saw the monumental tediousness of women's work,
and that it was, at the same time, exalted, thrilling and mesmerizing.
And then she moved into plays like *Conduct of Life* and *Mud*. I think
she's a great writer and the extent to which she's not appreciated
here or in England is an incredible crime and an act of racism. And
she's the only master playwright who's actually trained another
generation, so many wonderful writers like José Rivera, and Migdalia
Cruz and Eduardo Machado. And she's a great director.

And then Churchill is like ... God. The greatest living, English-
language playwright and, in my opinion, the most important
English-language playwright since Williams. There's nothing like
Fen or *Top Girls*. She came to see *Angels* at the National and I felt
hideously embarrassed. Suddenly it sounded like this huge Caryl
Churchill rip-off. She's a very big and obvious influence. One of the
things that I'm happy about with *Perestroika* is that it's bigger and
messier. I found a voice and it doesn't sound as much influenced by
Churchill as *Millennium*. The important thing about the British
socialist writers, even the ones that I find irritating, is that that style
comes out of the Berliner Ensemble touring through Britain. They
have a strong Marxist tradition they're not at war with and they've
found a way—Bond, of course, did it first—to write Marxist, socialist
theatre that has a connection with English-language antecedents. So

it was very important for me to read Brenton, Churchill, Hare and Edgar. During the late '70s, when there was nothing coming out of this country, they seemed to be writing all the good plays.

DS: Whenever I teach *Angels in America*, I start by noting how important it is that it *queers* America, the idea of America. As the subtitle makes plain, this is a play that deals with national themes and identities and recognizes that gay men have been at the centre of that. Although Queer Nation had not yet been formed when you started working on the play, I still see the play connected to its politics. How do you see *Angels* in relation to the development of queer politics?

TK: I'm in my late thirties now and of the generation that made ACT UP and then Queer Nation, a generation stuck between the people that made the '60s and their children. I see traces of the Stonewall generation, of Larry Kramer and even to a certain extent, Harvey Fierstein, but also the generation of Greg Araki and David Drake, that totally Queer Nation, Boy Bar kind of thing. (I have problems with both of them. I didn't like *The Living End* at all.) But I feel that I'm part of a group of people, Holly Hughes, David Greenspan ...

DS: Paula Vogel.

TK: And Paula. I told Don Shewey in the *Voice* that I think of it as a change from the Theatre of the Ridiculous to the Theatre of the Fabulous. The Queer Nation chant—"We're here. We're queer. We're fabulous. Get used to it."—uses fabulous in two senses. First, there's fabulous as opposed to ridiculous. It's amazing in *The Beautiful Room is Empty* when Edmund White writes about Stonewall being a ridiculous thing for these people. That's the essence of the ridiculous. It's a political gesture, what Wayne Koestenbaum calls "retaliatory self-invention," a gesture of defiance. And the drag gesture is still not completely capable of taking itself seriously. I don't want to talk in a judgmental way, but there's still a very heavy weight of self-loathing, I think, that's caught up in it. You couldn't say that Charles Ludlam was self-loathing. But there is a sense in which the masochism—I'm sounding like Louis now—and the flashes of really intense misogyny (when another victim of oppression is sneered at and despised because of her weakness) come from the fact that one hates one's own weakness. There's a certain embracing of weakness and powerlessness in the whole Ridiculous ...

DS: John Waters, too, is such a good example of that.

TK: Yes. And there's also an incompatibility with direct political discourse. How can you be that kind of queer and talk politics? And of course what AIDS forced on the community was the absolute necessity of doing that, of not becoming a drab old lefty, or old new lefty, of maintaining a queer identity and still being able to talk seriously about treatment protocols and oppression.

So there's fabulous in the sense of an evolutionary advance over the notion of being ridiculous, and fabulous also in the sense of being fabled, having a history. That's very important, that we now have a consciousness about where we come from in a way that John Vacarro and Charles Ludlam, when they were making it, pre-Stonewall, didn't have. Think back to Jack Smith, that whole tradition of which he was the most gorgeous and accomplished incarnation. Ludlam died before ACT UP started. Had he lived, there's no question but that he would have had no problem with it. I knew nothing about his theoretical writings when he was alive, I just knew he was the funniest man I'd ever seen. But he was working through a very strong politics and theory of the theatre and I'm sure the times would have made many amazing changes in his art. So I feel we're another step along the road now. It's incumbent upon us to examine history and be aware of history, of where we've come from and what has given us the freedom to talk the way we do now. We're the generation that grew up when homophobia wasn't axiomatic and universal and when the closet wasn't nailed shut and had to be kicked open.

DS: The progress narrative you're constructing here makes me think that *Perestroika*'s idea of history is not only rooted in dialectical materialism but also in your belief in the possibility of progress and enlightenment.

TK: As Walter Benjamin wrote, you have to be constantly looking back at the rubble of history. The most dangerous thing is to become set upon some notion of the future that isn't rooted in the bleakest, most terrifying idea of what's piled up behind you. Scattered through my plays is stuff from Tennessee Williams, Robert Patrick, all the gay writers that came before. When I started *Angels*, I started it, following Brecht, who always did this, as an answer: you find a play that makes you mad—either you love that it makes you mad or you think it's abominable—and needs to be responded to. I had seen *As Is* which I really hated (I hated the production even more than the play). I had seen so much bad gay theatre that all seemed so horrendously domestic. And it's even in *Torch Song*, although I really love *Torch Song*, which, obviously, is an important antecedent. When Arnold, who desires to be straight, turns to his mother and says, "I only want what you had," there's something that's really getting missed here.

When I started coming out of the closet in the early '80s, and was going to the Coalition for Lesbian and Gay Rights meetings, it was so bourgeois and completely devoid of any kind of left political critique. There was no sense of community with any other oppressed groups, just "let's get the gay rights bill passed in New York and have brunches and go to the gym." It was astonishing to discover that only ten years before there had been the Gay Activist's Alliance and the Lavender Left and hippie gay people and I thought, "What happened? Where did they go?" And of course they went with the '60s. But ACT UP changed all of that. Now it's hard for people to remember that there was a time before ACT UP, and that it burst violently and rapidly on the scene.

DS: It seems to me that this development of queer politics has in part prepared for the success of *Angels in America*.

TK: Absolutely. It kicked down the last door. The notion of acting up, much more than outing, is what really blew out liberal gay politics. I mean, you depend upon the work that's done by the slightly assimilationist but hard-working, libertarian, civil rights groups, like the NAACP, but then at some point you need the Panthers. You need a group that says, "Enough of this shit. This is going too slow. And if we don't see some big changes now, we're going to cause trouble. We really are here. Get used to it." Up until that point, the American majority—if there is such a thing—fantasizes that the noise will just go away, that it's a trend. The way the play talks, and its complete lack of apology for that kind of fagginess, is something that would not have made sense before.

DS: Unlike *Torch Song*, in which Arnold just wants to be normal, *Angels in America*, along with queer theory and politics, calls into question the category of the normal.

TK: Right.

DS: This is what I mean by queering America: there is no such thing in this text as a natural sexuality.

TK: When I met you at TCG and was so stupid about Eve Sedgwick's *Between Men*, you suggested I go back and look at it again. And I did. And then *Epistemology of the Closet* came out and what she's saying is true for all oppressed groups in this country. This project of pushing the margin to the centre is really the defining project, not just for her, but for bell hooks and Cornel West and so many feminist writers. Creating the fiction of the white, normal, straight male centre has been the defining project of American history. I'm working on a play about slavery and reading 18th century texts and it has been the central preoccupation in American politics for the entire time during which this land has been trying to make itself into a country. The founding fathers weren't getting up and arguing about making homosexuality legal, but it's been an ongoing issue. And in this century, as you point out in your book, it's been an obsession during various times of crisis. It always seems to me to be the case that in the concerns of any group called a minority and called oppressed can be found the biggest problems and the central identity issues that the country is facing. Also, because of Brecht, when I was writing *Bright Room* and reading the history of the collapse of the Weimar Republic, I realized that the key is the solidarity of the oppressed for the oppressed—being able to see the connecting lines—which is one of the things that AIDS has done, because it's made disenfranchisement incredibly clear across colour lines and gender lines.

DS: Which is why the play also goes in a sense beyond the identity politics of the 1970s. Or rather, it's interrogating identity politics and attempting to valorize coalition politics.

TK: I think that's a good way to put it. There's still a lot to be explored in identity politics and for me one of the big questions in *Perestroika* is: what exactly does a community mean and what kind of threat does somebody like Roy Cohn pose to the notion of identity politics?

DS: One scene that I found very interesting in regard to that is the one in which Louis confronts Joe about his legal briefs and broaches the idea of lesbians and gays as a class.

TK: There's an amazing term in constitutional law: suspect class. It isn't a community of like-minded people with similar material interests, as in the working class, but rather a group that has been formed, to a certain degree, by hostility from without. From the point of view of the constitution, the forces that shape the group into a class are suspect rather than the people in the class. I find that a fascinating idea. In America, you can always talk about social justice but never economic justice. There is no such thing—supposedly—as economic class in this country. So there's a community that seems to be incredibly clear at times and then at other moments, depending on which way the light is striking, disappears completely.

DS: You were talking before about Brecht and the importance of a materialist analysis. In your work, however, there's a much more indirect relationship between culture and the workings of capitalism.

TK: We're in a different time. And, of course, the clearer Brecht gets, the more trouble he gets into. The closer he is to Trotsky and the further away he is from Lenin, the better he is.

There's also a question in Brecht of historical agency and subjectivity: are we the subjects of history or are we completely subject to history? Do we make it or are we made by it? That's not certainty. And with *Arturo Ui*, it's a miracle that in the middle of it he could see it all happening so clearly. But finally it's unsatisfying because Hitler was in many cases supported by the proletariat, so something else was going on. And now we're in a period of such profound confusion, it's certainly impossible to be a Marxist now. It's almost impossible even to be a socialist.

DS: Why do you think it's impossible to be a Marxist now?

TK: I don't want to start sounding like the more right-wing perestroikans from Russia, but I do think that we really have to ask questions about the notion of violent revolution as the locomotive of history. And that is in Marx. Of course being a Marxist is an odd idea to start with … was Luxemburg a Marxist or a communist or social-ist or was she a … Luxemburgan? And you read people like Luxemburg and Benjamin and the weirdos and rejects and those are the people who speak now, even Trotsky in his exile days. Although there are things in Marx that are still of incalculable value.

DS: It seems to me that it's useful to distinguish between Marxism as a political program and Marxism as a mode of analysis. Isn't the latter indispensable?

TK: Yes, if you mean dialectical materialism. I think that rigorous, classical dialectical materialism is probably of great value. But any method of analysis that becomes Jesuitical is problematic. And con-sider that some of the most powerful political movements of the 20th century have been led by people who were not materialists. Martin Luther King was not a materialist. He was a Baptist minister. Libera-tion theology is in some ways a materialist interpretation of the

Gospels, but in other ways it's founded on notions of sacrifice, for instance, that are profoundly lacking in Marx.

It's difficult to separate out the political Marx from the theoretical Marx. In the parts of *Capital* that I've read and in some of the early Marx, he talks about things that are not purely materialist forces. He actually uses words like magic, spirit and soul in *The Economic and Philosophic Manuscripts*. So a Marxist-Leninism that rejects the spiritual world is something we have to be very skeptical about. Take Yugoslavia. There must be a way of analyzing what's happening in the Balkans in a historical materialist fashion. But I also can't help but think—and maybe it's just because I'm sloppy—that there's something else going on. You start to think in a kind of new age-y way about energies in the world. Brecht did, and you can see that in his poetry. There's injustice everywhere and no rebellion. I think Adorno was really wrong: after Auschwitz we need poetry all the more because you can't talk about these things except by recourse to forms of expression that are profoundly unscientific.

DS: That really ties in with Benjamin and the conjunction between the political and religious, Marxism and Judaism. His politicization of Messianic time as Utopia is absolutely crucial to your project.

TK: And his sense of utopianism is also so profoundly apocalyptic: a teleology, but not a guarantee. Or a guarantee that Utopia will be as fraught and as infected with history. It's not pie in the sky at all.

DS: I keep thinking of that line from the "Angelus Novus:" "Where we perceive a chain of events, [the angel] sees one single catastrophe which keeps piling wreckage upon wreckage and hurls it in front of his feet." The scene in heaven in *Perestroika* really took my breath away, seeing the wreckage behind the scrim.

TK: And there's a whole scene that we didn't perform because it just didn't play: they're listening on an ancient radio to the first report of the disaster at Chernobyl. And these are very Benjaminian, Rilkean angels. I think that is also a very American trope. In *The American Religion*, Harold Bloom keeps referring to this country as the evening land, where the promise of Utopia is so impossibly remote that it brings one almost to grieving and despair. Seeing what heaven looks like from the depths of hell. It's the most excruciating pain, and even as one is murdering and rampaging and slashing and burning to achieve Utopia, one is aware that the possibility of attaining Utopia is being irreparably damaged. People in this country knew somewhere what they were doing, but as we moved into this century, we began to develop a mechanism for repressing that knowledge. There's a sense of progress, but at tremendous cost. What will never be.

DS: And it's Prior who carries the burden of that in *Angels*.

TK: Yes.

DS: And of course embedded even in his name is the sense that he's out of step with time, both too soon and belated, connected to the past and future, to ancestors and what's to come.

TK: He's also connected to Walter Benjamin. I've written about my friend Kimberly [Flynn] who is a profound influence on me. And she and I were talking about this utopian thing that we share—she's the person who introduced me to that side of Walter Benjamin. The line that he wrote that's most important to her—and is so true—is, "even the dead will not be safe if the enemy wins." She said jokingly that at times she felt such an extraordinary kinship with him that she thought she was Walter Benjamin reincarnated. And so at one point in the conversation, when I was coming up with names for my characters, I said, "I had to look up something in Benjamin—not you, but the prior Walter." That's where the name came from. I had been looking for one of those WASP names that nobody gets called anymore.

DS: Despite all these utopian longings, at the centre of both *Bright Room* and *Angels* are characters, Agnes and Louis, who are, in one way or another, liberals. I realize that *Angels* is not about Louis, but structurally he is at the centre; he's the one who ties all the characters together. Not that his viewpoint is the prevailing one.

TK: Right.

DS: So in both plays you've foregrounded well-intentioned liberals whose actions are at an extraordinary remove from their intentions. And of course we know from Brecht, among others, that ethics are always defined by action. Why did you put these characters at the centre?

TK: I've never thought of Louis and Agnes as a pair but they really are. I think they're very American. American radicalism has always been anarchic as opposed to socialist. The socialist tradition in this country is so despised and has been blamed so much on immigrants. It's been constructed as a Jewish, alien thing, which is not the way socialism is perceived anywhere else in the world, where there is a native sense of communities that we don't share. What we have is a native tradition of anarchism. And that's such a fraught, problematic tradition because Ronald Reagan is as much the true heir as Abbie Hoffman. Abbie Hoffman was an anarcho-communist and Ronald Reagan is an ego-anarchist. But they're both anarchists. And anarchism is a tradition I have a lot of trouble with.

The strain in the American character that I feel the most affection for and that I feel has the most potential for growth is American liberalism, which is incredibly short of what it needs to be and incredibly limited and exclusionary and predicated on all sorts of racist, sexist, homophobic and classist prerogatives. And yet, as Louis asks, why has democracy succeeded in America? And why does it have this potential, as I believe it does? I really believe that there is the potential for radical democracy in this country, one of the few places on earth where I see it as a strong possibility. It doesn't seem to be happening in Russia. There is a tradition of liberalism, of a kind of social justice, fair play and tolerance—and each of these things is problematic and can certainly be played upon in the most horrid ways. Reagan kept the most hair-raising anarchist aspects of his agenda hidden and presented himself as a good old-fashioned liberal who kept invoking FDR. It may just be sentimentalism on my part because I am the child of liberal-pinko parents, but I do believe in it—as much as I often find it despicable. It's sort of like the Democratic National Convention every four years: it's horrendous and you can feel it sucking all the energy from progressive movements in this country, with everybody pinning their hopes on this sleazy bunch of guys. But you do have Jesse Jackson getting up and calling the Virgin Mary a single mother, and on an emotional level, and I hope also on a more practical level, I do believe that these are the people in whom to have hope. I mean, I don't want to get paternalistic about it either. And Agnes is, as her name says, an egg. She is unformed, while Louis is a much more ... the characters are very different. But I feel that these are the people whom the left either can hook onto and mobilize, or not.

I feel that in Germany in the late '20s, these were the group of people who came out and voted Communist in that one election before Hindenburg blew it for everybody. Their genuine good nature, their fear, lack of insight and weakness were played upon, and the left did not find a way to speak to them. Louis is a gay version of that whom ACT UP could have enrolled and then radicalized. And I do feel that ACT UP did that. Now we'll see how lasting it is.

DS: Although none of the characters is involved with mass movement politics.

TK: But the play is set—and I think this is very important—when
there's no such thing in the United States for generally progressive
people. For someone like Belize, there isn't anything. The Rainbow
Coalition has started to waffle and fall apart. And there is nothing in
the gay community. There's the Gay Pride parade, and GMHC and
going up every year and getting humiliated at the City Council in
Newark. '84–'85 was a horrible, horrible time. It really seemed like
the maniacs had won for good. What Martin says in *Millennium* now
seems like a joke that we can all snigger at, but at the time, I just
wrote what I thought was most accurate. The Republicans had lost
the Senate but would eventually get that back because the South
would go Republican. There would never be a Democratic president
again because Mondale was the best answer we could make to
Ronald Reagan, the most popular president we've ever had. So none
of these people had anything they could hook into, which is the
history of the left. When the moment comes, when the break happens and history can be made, do we step in and make it or do we
flubber and fail? As much as I am horrified by what Clinton does—
and we could have had someone better—we didn't completely blow
it this time.

DS: I'm interested in father-son relationships in the play—the way
that Roy is set up as the son of a bad father, Joseph McCarthy, and
how he, in turn, is a bad father to Joe. And the scene between Roy
and Joe is juxtaposed against the S&M scene between Louis and the
Man in the park. But isn't that S&M dynamic really crucial for
mapping so many of the relationships in the play? Both Louis and
Harper seem amazingly masochistic, in very different ways.

TK: I hope that the two scenes speak to each other in the right
balance. I don't know if you've read Dale Peck's book, *Martin and
John*. It's extraordinary. He's one of the few gay writers I've read who
really deals with the issue of the father in gay life, as opposed to the
mother. A lot of what he does is to play variations on father-son
relationships, the father as a sexualized identity. There are things
that I wanted to tackle with that, though. I want to explore S&M
more because I feel that it's an enormously pervasive dynamic, that
it's inextricably wound up with issues of patriarchy and that there
are ways in which it plays through every aspect of life. I think it's

something that needs to be understood, thought about and spoken about more openly.

DS: I agree, that's why I've been writing about the relationship between masculinity and masochism in our culture.

TK: We subjects of capitalist societies have to talk about the ways in which we are constructed to eroticize and cathect pain, as well as the way pain is transformed into pleasure, and self-destruction into self-creation. What price must we finally pay for that? I'm glad you're writing about it. Until now, there's been a kind of dumb liberation politics—all forms of sexual practice are off-limits for analysis and GSMA is fine, we just leave it in the bedroom. But of course it's not just the kind of S&M that's acted out that needs to concern us. I think that sexuality should still be subject to analysis, including the question of why we're gay instead of straight, which I think has nothing to do with the hypothalamus or interstitial brain cells, but has to do with trauma.

DS: But isn't all sexuality rooted in trauma?

TK: We're just good Freudians. Yes, it's all trauma and loss and the question is, are there specific forms of trauma? I believe that there is an etiology of sexuality that's traceable if anybody wants to spend the money on an analyst. Oedipus is still legitimate grounds for exploration and inquiry. And I think that the notion of the cultural formation of personalities is of tremendous importance. In another sense, I really feel that it was incredibly important that Roy's generation of gay men have that kind of deeply patriarchal, gender-enforced notion of the seduction of youth, the ephebe and the elder man. Unbelievably, we still see that popping up in the plays of certain people whose names I won't mention. All the older gay man wants is the younger gay man. That comes down from the Greeks, homosexuality being a form of tutelage, of transmission, of dominance and submission. It felt to me that that would absolutely be part of Roy's repressed, ardent desire for Joe. And then what you see replicated in the blessing scene is a form of love which has to flow through inherited structures of hierarchical power.

These are some of the oldest questions with which we've been torturing ourselves: what is the relationship between sexuality and power? And is sexuality merely an expression of power? And is there even such a thing as a sexuality? Do we all want to end up like John Stoltenberg married to Andrea Dworkin? Is male sexuality always aggressive? What do we make of the Phallus? And then, what's to be made of notions like the lesbian Phallus? And how do we escape it? Any inquiry into that speaks to the larger questions which for me are really the most exciting, interesting and difficult ones: if we buy into the notion of the construction of these forms of behaviour, and the construction of personalities that engage in these behaviours, do we believe in the deconstruction of these forms? What is that deconstruction? There's the issue of reforming the personality to become a socialist subject, starting with the trash that capitalism has made of us. And people who are formed in the image of the individual ego ... how do we remake that ego in a way that isn't itself masochistic? Is there a form of unmaking that isn't destructive?

This is why I'm so fascinated by Brecht's *lehrstück* plays. The *Baden-Baden* play: by what process, that isn't submission, does the individual ego become part of a collective? All that Brecht can arrive at is death and submission. It's that very experimental form he was working in before he had to leave Germany and decided to become Brecht-the-genius-writer-of-canonical-literature instead. A pilot and a group of mechanics are flying and their plane crashes in the desert and they're perched between life and death. They ask a chorus of learned Marxist-Leninists—who are the audience—should they live or should they die? And there are a series of illustrations asking, Does man help his fellow man? And the mechanics, who represent the working class, consent to being part of the necessity of history and live because of their consent. That is, they die and are reborn. But the pilot, who is an individual, is destroyed. He's dismantled. He refuses to die and so they have to kill him over and over again. The repetition is kind of creepy Stalinist, but what he's getting at is the absolute refusal, the marvelousness of the individual ego, and the pain and torment with which we imagine taking it apart. Is there a process other than revolution, other than bloodshed, agony and pain—which is fundamentally masochistic—by which we can transform ourselves into socialist subjects? That's a big question and it turns you toward things like Zen.

DS: That's the question of the play: what is there beyond pain? Is Utopia even imaginable?

TK: And the loss. It's the thing that I don't understand at all, which I think is undertheorized and underrepresented in the problematics of the left. If our lives are in fact shaped by trauma and loss—and as I get older it seems to me that life is very, very profoundly shaped by loss and death—how do you address that? And how does one progress in the face of that? That's the question that the AIDS epidemic has asked. Because there is nothing more optimistic than America, in the most awful way (like "up with people!"). It makes so many people queasy and it's the subject of so much sarcasm because it seems so dumb. But identity is shaped, even racial identity. If there weren't bigots, there wouldn't be a politics of race. That there has to be a politics of difference speaks to the presence of enormous oppression and violence and terror. What do we do? It's an interesting thing because the more we know about history, the more we realize—and this is an important thing about sadomasochism—that it really does return, it never ends. You can just see in our present moment a thousand future Sarajevos. You just know that when you're ninety, if you live so long, they'll still be fighting. Even after the Holocaust, the monsters are still among us. And can you forgive? That's why I ask this question of forgiveness because its possibility is also, I think, undertheorized and underexpressed.

DS: Relating to the question of forgiveness, why do you use Mormons in the play, along with Jews? Because the angels are so clearly Old Testament angels, angels of the vengeful God. How does that tie in with the Mormon religion?

TK: There are interesting similarities between Mormonism and Judaism. They both have a very elusive notion of damnation. It's always been unclear to me, as a Jew, what happens if you don't do good things. Presumably you don't go to Paradise. There is a hell but, even among the Orthodox, there isn't an enormous body of literature about it—it's not like Catholicism. Mormonism has a hell but it has three layers of heaven, four actually, that I know of. Also, Mormonism is a diasporic religion. And as far as I'm concerned, the most interesting thing about Judaism is the whole diasporic, secular culture.

Mormonism is of the book. It draws its strength very much from the literal, physical volume, which isn't sacred like the Torah, but it's all about the discovery of a book. They say that Joseph Smith had a Hebrew teacher who was a Rabbi. Also, Judaism, like Mormonism, is not a religion about redemption based on being sorry for what you've done and asking for forgiveness. The hallmark of Mormonism is, "By deeds ye shall be known." As you said, ethics are defined by action. And that is also true in Judaism. Your intentions make very little difference to God. What counts is what you do and whether you're righteous in your life. That appeals to me. It also feels very

American. I wanted to have an orthodox religion that someone was having a lot of trouble with but I didn't want Orthodox Judaism. And I wanted something American.

I started the play with an image of an angel crashing through a bedroom ceiling and I knew that this play would have a connection to American themes. So the title, *Angels in America*, came from that. And I think the title, as much as anything else, suggested Mormons because the prototypical American angel is the angel Moroni. It's of this continent, the place that Jesus visited after he was crucified. It's like Blake and the New Jerusalem. Christ was here and this continent does have some tendrils snaking back into biblical mythology. It's a great story—not the Book of Mormon which, as Mark Twain said, is chloroform in print—but the story of Joseph Smith's life and the trek, the gathering of Zion. That's so American. The idea of inventing a complete cosmology out of a personal vision is something I can't imagine a European doing. I guess Swedenborg and Blake sort of did that but it didn't become this theocratic empire. And unlike Swedenborg, which is rather elegant and beautiful, and Blake, which is extraordinarily beautiful but mostly incomprehensible, it's so dumb. It's so naive and disingenuous. It's like Grandma Moses, the celestial and the terrestrial heavens, with all this masonry incorporated into it. It's so American Gothic. I wanted Mormons in this play. I find their immense industry, diligence and faith moving. The symbol of Utah and of the Mormon kingdom of God is a beehive, which is, in its own way, a socialist, communist image. And there were a lot of experiments in Utah of communally-owned property, which is what Joseph Smith originally dictated, with wealth held in common, and experiments with controlled economies. Their social experiments were independent of, but similar to, European socialist, communal notions of the 19th century.

Now, they're so right-wing and horrible. Although the Mormons I've met I've actually sort of liked. I've found something dear and nice about them—they have good strong families, with all the horror that that implies. But I think, as with Judaism, there's not an enormously high incidence of grotesque abuses of patriarchal power, incest or wife-beating, for example. So they come out as nice people with centres while most conservatives are so horrendous. When I was working on Joe, I wanted to write a conservative man that I actually liked. I didn't finally succeed [laughs]. Although I feel that he gets somewhere and will ultimately be redeemable, in *Angels*, part three.

Along with bits and pieces of Mormonism, I used the Kabbala for the angels. They're mostly from Holy Scripture and the Kabbala, except in their method of delivering the epistle—purely Mormon. The idea of a man who gets a set of spectacles from an angel—only in America: *The Fly* as theology.

DS: And you're working with Robert Altman now?

TK: Yes, to turn *Angels* into an Altman movie.

DS: You're writing the screenplay.

TK: Yes.

DS: After seeing *Short Cuts*, I realized why.

TK: *Nashville* had a profound impact on me, the extraordinary interweaving of stories. I wanted somebody whom I respected and whom I knew would make it very unlike the stage play. And I'm completely confident of that [laughs]. He allows a certain kind of messiness to be a part of his aesthetic, which appeals to me a lot. He's the first filmmaker, years before Woody Allen, to go for that hand-held camera, documentary look. When I first approached him about it, I hoped that he might be interested in doing it for television, but he felt that was chicken-shit [laughs]. And I'm sure he's the only person in Hollywood who said immediately that we have to do two films.

I hope that I can get him to deal with the difficult question of gay sexuality. He hasn't always been great about that. But I can't believe that he'd want to do this without being aware that there are going to be men naked in bed together, or in the park. I really want him not to get silly about that because I'll just die if this is another one of those films with two men lying in bed with the bedsheet pulled up against their pecs. I think it will be very important, given the way that he improvises, that he has some gay actors in the cast. I don't want to see a lot of straight people trying to figure out what it's like.

DS: And you're working on another play?

TK: I haven't completely committed myself to what the next big one is going to be. But I have two that are cooking. One is about Vermeer; it's sort of a history of capitalism. And the other is a play about a slave named Henry Box Brown who mailed himself out of slavery in a box to Philadelphia. Then I discovered in a fluke that Henry Box Brown wound up in England and toured English textile towns trying to get them to boycott Southern cotton before the War.

When I was working on *Millennium* at the National, I went to one of the towns and I've just unearthed this whole treasure chest of amazing characters from the Industrial Revolution.

It's the international character of capital, that slavery was made profitable because the British imported 800 million tons of cotton a year for the biggest textile mills in the world. When the blockade was set up, the textile towns were hit with a famine the likes of which Britain had never seen before. It was total economic devastation because of the American Civil War. A great evil does not exist in the world independent of support.

When I visited the town, I went to research the man who had owned the biggest textile mill in all of England. He was also a liberal in Parliament and passed the first labour laws in Britain. And he had a whole family of what sound like great bleeding-heart liberals that made millions of pounds off of cotton. One of them even married a mill girl, so she's shown all over the town standing on ears of corn, and he built her a castle on a hill which is now in ruins. And I found my way into the castle, and in the central hall are roundels over each door in which are bas-relief depictions of cotton being grown in America—horrendous scenes of white men whipping black people and black people in chains, all in the most damning detail. And his wife became an outrageous alcoholic, embarrassed him for years and finally drank herself to death. That great little tragedy has also been mixed into the play. And George Wolfe is going to direct it both here and at the National, probably with British white actors and African-American actors.

DS: So you remain committed to writing history plays.

TK: I'm a little nervous about it because I think that *Angels* is my best play because I started writing about my world. But there's a kind of safety in writing a history play—you can make up everything. And it insulates you to a certain extent from the assault of everyday life. But I've also decided to write more *Angels in America* plays and those may be the only ones in which I deal with contemporary reality.

When I was writing *Perestroika* this summer, I got very, very angry at the characters. At first, I thought it was because I was sick of them, but now I've come to realize that I hated the idea of not being able to work on them anymore. I want to know what happens to them. I already have most of the plot of part three in my head. It won't be continuous, but I could have a cycle of nine or ten plays by the time I'm done. The characters will get older as I get older. I'll be bringing in new ones and letting characters like Roy go. So, I'm excited about that. I think it's harder to write that kind of play than a history play.

DS: Although I think of *Angels in America* as a history play.

TK: In a sense it is. Although when I started writing it, it wasn't. But it receded into the past. As it gets older, it will become increasingly about a period of history. There is a danger for me of writing too much out of books because I'm sort of socially awkward and not much of an adventurer. I don't want to write only about the past. Brecht never wrote anything about his contemporaries. Did he?

DS: *Arturo Ui*.

TK: Except it's set in Chicago and they're speaking in a very different way.

DS: What about the learning plays?

TK: But again, they're drowned in pseudo-Confucian poetry and set in China and other places.

DS: But in all of his work he was historicizing his particular moment.

TK: Exactly. That's all you can ever do.